ANGELGOONZ

ANGELGOONZ

MELVIN SHOALES

CONTENTS

IF "SATAN" HAS SOME "GANGSTERS"?
"GOD" GOTS "SOME" GOONZ"
ANGEL'GOONZ "BY MINISTER" MELVIN"APDTA"

…….THE BEGINING…..

"WE NEVER LEFT OUR "LAND" THOSE OF US THAT WERE ALREADY OVER HERE IN THEE "AMERICAS" BEFORE ANYONE ELSE.

THERE WAS THE BEGINING THE "BLACK"AFRICAN" WE "HOWEVER "LEFT TO FIGHT "THE "GULLAH"WARS".

"FROM" THE "BLACKNESS" OF "SPACE'DEEP WITHIN THE"COSMOS" TO THE "EARTH" THE "OPPOSITE" OF "BLACK" WAS 'ORDAINED" TO "RULE'6000" YEARS"1885 EUROPEANS ENDED UP "CONQUERING" "MOTHER "AFRICA"..

More Importantly to Note Is that the letter " J" wasn't invented until about 400 years ago But I Ask You The "Reader" A Very Important

"Question"? How long Have "Africans" Black" As "Solomon" "People" been Black Brown Dark As Smoke"? How long has our So Journey Been In "SLAVERY"? Past "SLAVERY" AND MODERN And Present??? The New SLAVERY is the 3 Strike Law Prison Stock Market Privatizing Prisons on "The inmate Stock "Market" The 13 TH AMENDMENT Makes It "Crystal "Clear" The LONG RANGE SCHEMERS THEY TRULY ARE And Exactly What we are Dealing with Mainly Started with "Christianity "As A Way To "Wickedly "Control "Slaves "Nothing "More" Than

"SATANS" GANGSTERS* OF " HELL "MART" And For ALL THE "HELL'MODERN" DAY" BABALON"BABALON" MODERN" DAY'BABALON"

" THE "UNITED"STATES'OF"AMERICA" "SATANS' GANGSTERS" CAUSES. GOD" To RAISE SOME GOONZ......"ANGEL'GOONZ" BY "MR MINISTER MELVIN APDTA"

My Own Studies Digging And digging Inquiries ONLY "WHITE LIVES MATTER" Our Children "ATE" TREE BARK AND DIRT we must always under Darkness Praise God Enough To See The Light Of Day Another Day Over White Supremacy It Is Their" Direct Fear" Of Blacks Returning To Our Original Place Of Spirituality

Of The Best Religion WHICH is to "DO UNTO OTHERS. AS YOU WILL HAVE THEM DO UNTO YOU" And Whites Are Not Primarily Concerned with Reparations Because They Know Many Of Us Were Already over Here

IN THE Americas BUT THAT DON'T MEAN CRAP" WE ALL STILL DESERVE REPARATIONS" SINCE 'SATAN" Got Some " Gangsters"?

"GOD"GOT"SOME"GOONZ"ANGEL GOONZ"

INTRO #2

As A Black Nation Of Great People, we know that we must be Thankful to God in Heaven Each Day for the supreme opportunity to live our lives And learn And Grow to be better Thinkers And Better people than we were before each day At a Time to Know that "OUR" PAST"Doesnt need us But, Our Future does" its crazy because whites and brainwashed blacks desire to continue to ignore All The "Systemic Racism that goes on every day in these united snakes of America Who robbed us of our culture and are imitators of the original Success of The Black Man Black woman And Black Child to destroy us All are seriously I must admit after realizing "Egypt" is Right here In America. I Begin to go deep President Trump who God Has put in Power for a reason NOBODY DESERVES TO BE PUT IN A HIGH POSITION LIKE THAT AND, COMMIT TREA-

SON"AFRICA" ISNT A "SHIT HOLE" AS TRUMP SUGGESTS BUT, THE BEGINING OF ALL LIFE AND, RICHES ANYWAY NOBODY CAN GET CLOSE ENOUGH TO THE KING TO HURT THE KING TO TRY AND ASSASSINATE THE KING WITHOUT THOSE CLOSET TO THE "KING" To "GREEN"LIGHT" The "Hit. .We Must Learn To Appreciate And Love Our Kings." I Pray God Helps Us And keeps us safe. This Racism runs deep in hate from The "Mother whore" in Black Communities in Our History From White supremacy However, Like I Say

"Our History Does Not Have to Determine Our Future Or Destiny." I'm Considered A giraffe In a Sense I Don't Lower My Head To NOTHING BUT THE TRUTH "Black Life Is so Cheap With Poverty Spirits And It's Sad Because Our The Voting really do create a False Sense of Illusion Of False Power

black Woman is not Respected Or honored Enough It All reaks of Powerful White supremacy

And we must OVERSTAND That our opposition "OREO SO"CALLED FRIEND "OR "FOE" "WHITE HO" The "Mother Whore" Does not desire our full and complete Freedom Without "NO TRICKNOLOGY" ATTACHED They only Function ON AND UNDER TRICKNOLOGY" And TRICKS ARE FOR "KIDS" THEY Know THAT. And it's Very Very Very Very Very "Imperative" That We

"OVERSTAND" That "RUSSIA" Is Very Much Apart Of The White Supremacy Through Its "Eastern European States" With Different "Flags" Representing "The Same" OBJECTIVE" New World Order Crushing The Blacks Make it look Like Its ALL Them ONLY Doing It To Themselves As If "WHITE POWERE ISNT DIRECTLY INVOLVED" But it Was The Honorable President Putin to Reveal the true Christ White Supremacy Hate the cat being out of the bag Concerning The true color of Our Christ. MAY GOD BLESS PRESIDENT PUTIN . America is falling because of her treatment of her "Slave$"

Of The original People African People of The Original World And MELANIN Is a Substance We Africans Are Full Of ABORIGNAL People of the Land Of Mother Africa There is a struggle a Complete Sick Struggle of power between Russia and The MOTHER WHORE AMERICA BABALON BABALON THE ONCE GREAT CITY "COUNTRY" Is Falling NOW" as we Speak She Is Losing Everything From God In Heaven Because, Of her love for "Black"&" Poor" thirst of Blood and, Her love for satan the mother whores god. To Gain From Satan Their god to and to Hell. WE must Stand on Truth ALONE.ALONE.ALONE.ALONE.ALONE. And On Our Own Two "FEET" We Must Stop Waiting On Whites To Continue To Handicap Us We Can Do This It's All" Mental "And We All Been Mentally Messed Up Passed Down Genetically Through The Mitochondrial DNA

Through The Black Woman Along with Complete Fear Of The Devil The Real ONE with blue eyes and Then OREO COOKIE "Modern Day "Contact"Lenses"Black Woman Want To Wear Light Blue EYES NOT realizing its blue the RECESSIVE GENE In THE DNA IS WEAK SUPREMELY WEAK" And SHE Think They Mentally Good Not Wanting To Be What She was "BORN" TO BE "The dominant"&"WEAK ASS BROTHERS TOO WANNA BE WHITE;. Crazy in Its self Not Wanting To Be What God Made You. But "Yacub"Made And Produced The Recessive Gene Race To Take Over And Get Rid Of Spirituality Our Original GOD IS DO ONTO OTHERS AS WE WOULD

HAVE THEM DO ONTO "US" And THIS IS "COMPLETE SUBMISSION TO THE WILL OF GOD" WHICH JUST SO HAPPENS TO BE "ISLAM" Is The LAMB ISLAM B=Black Black = The Dark Melanin Gene Activate The PINEAL GLAND" We Must Develop our Own Ideologies for

Entrepreneurship For Our Own Advancement Our UNITY So DISUNITY FOR WHITE SUPREMACY THINKERS AND NEW WORLD ORDER OF BLACKS 1ST Then RULE With Everyone Else That Assisted Greatly In the BLACK AFRICAN HOLOCAUST UNLIKE THE JEWISH HOLOCAUST 1941 to 1945 OUR HOLOCAUST WAS OVER 500 YEARS AND

COUNTING MODERN DAY HOLOCAUST AND CHEESENIP CHEEZITS ACTIVITIES But , "CRACKER"It All Comes From The CRACKLING OF THE "WHIP". we Must "OVERSTAND" THAT THE TRUTH DOESNT NEED NO DAMN HELP" ITS SOPPOSE TO SET US FREE ACCORDING TO THE SO CALLED "HOLY"BIBLE" WE AS A BLACK PEOPLE THE ONES THAT ARE NOT "BOOTY LICKERS AND "BACKSTABBERZ"OREO-COOKIES" WE MUST GO TO Work on a plan before a plan go to work on Us" White Gangsters" White Gangsters" in Government 'Suits' Sinse $atan" Got Sum Gangsters/'He do. !!!!!"GOD IN HEAVEN GOTS SOME GOONZ ON "EARTH"SOME YOU SEE" SOME" YOU DONT SEE BUT, YOU WILL SEE"SOON"ANGEL-GOONZ" OF

ALMIGHTY"GOD"IN "HEAVEN" FROM "THE "HOUSE "UNDER "GOD" IN "HEAVEN". ANGEL_GOONZ INTRO #2 By Melvin Shoales S.H.O.A.L.E.S." MEANS STRONGLY" HOLDING" ON" ALWAYS "LEARNING" "EVADING" "STRESS" BY THE GRACE OF GOD "ANGEL-GOONZ"

..........TRICKNOLOGY............

THEY TOOK A LOT OUT OF THE ORIGINAL BIBLE LIKE "GODS"TO GOD"

So as it is written in many of these "tampered" with Bibles they continue to revise. We know the Jehovah's Witness version, their own Bible, was written and revised. It also refers to the Hebrew scriptures and was released in the years 1953, 1955, 1957, 1958, and finally in 1960. Once all the "bootlickers" and "Oreo cookie" pastors sold out their own Black community to convene with the so-called former but current slave masters to this day.

However, we understand and now overstand all this HYPOCRISY is ultimately to control God's original aboriginal people, the lost tribe of "Shabazz" The Real Children Of Israel. But angel goonz were and, are present even in those days to fight for our causes and life. However, white supremacy desires to eliminate the melaninated people of God, and so we have good white people who desire the truth of it all. These whites ride with blacks and are considered niggers too.But none Of Us Are N#ggers We ARE Lovers Of God In Heaven And His Christ interestingly Enough

In Jude, I remind you of the angels who didn't stay" within the limits" of the Almighty God in Heaven. That's right, And, they left the place where they belonged. Also in Jude 16: "These are murmurers, complainers, walking after their own lusts, and their mouth speaks great swelling words, having men's persons in admiration because of their advantage over us, lost now found somewhat blacks here in the Americas, including us that were already over here to begin with."

God has written the great judgment. This we know. The "fallen angels" are there and here now. "Skeletons Remains" have always been found on Earth. Kept in chains of darkness is where the souls of the Nephilim, all of the hell of Hell, is here because of the Nephilim, evil of the fallen angels. It is so ironic that through my extensive research, the color of these beings was "chalky" As Soon As Their "Melaninated Spiritual Bodies" Touched The Worldly World ."MOTHER"EARTH"And because God says He knows what we know not.

As for teaching all this evil lawlessness, And; Lawlessness committing all this hell on Earth to the Earth people they taught, somehow cast them out from the very presence of Almighty God in Heaven, where they were all originally black like they were when "I"visited the "wheel". To some on Earth and even with the battles very forthcoming, we lost. So we lost Because Of Our trusting And, Loving The Enemy instead of Listening To God In Heaven The real Spirit Of God And,Only unity With God can Help Save black people, They have Mishandled The Blessings of God with The Money Filthy rich was The "Mother Whore" Now america is Broke so money She prints out of thin air because nothing's backing it but, Satan's American gangsters of white supremacy.

...."SATANS"GANSTERS".....

With guns and ancient technology they stole from "us" before putting us to sleep, black people and good white people. But good white people still have "white privilege" when they play their cards right." I've come to understand through the pineal gland that these white gangsters over the government mean business—Satan's business. They are a race of diluted versions on purpose from Satan from the original man, the black man and woman of the original Earth, not the metaverse.

The only way to make the original man hate himself and his woman is to pollute and dilute him and create a new race of devils to take over. "Everywhere they go, they don't leave." While God is constantly raising up messiahs to come through "Hip-hop" to help save us all, that's why all races love it. They are supposed to love it, the loving side of why the real reason God invented it, to fight white supremacy. They Corrupted "HipHop" Turning It "To Hate And The promotion of Murder And, Genocide From "Conscious"Life"Upliftment of Life" Saving"&"Loving "each other with Loving education of True Love"Rap"To"Death"Rap"

These smart white Jewish executives over this music allow its distribution of low evil frequency, low vibrational wicked frequencies, to go on and on over 25-30+ years to "premeate"The Take-Over"the Conscious" airwaves to promote the genocide and killing, robbing everything God in Heaven says don't do. America says do. "They could Have changed" the narrative years ago if they truly wanted or desired to truly be their brother's keeper. But, they are not your brother; they are from a completely different mother, Yacub's"grafted"Race".It Gets Deeper And, Deeper Mating the Lighter with the lighter Skinned People tampering with science Until they With The Fallen Angels Until they achieved their fathers wishes to get back at God in Heaven for kicking them out of Heaven they produced their supreme White race to forever Kill Steal And,Destroy The opposite of Their new race it is imperative to note that once you have been Kicked out of Heaven being Once "Angels"

You are no longer original once you've been diluted and polluted. Imposter Jews. Jesus says in the Bible, "I know those that say they are the original Jews and are not" You imposter jews are from The devil Your father satan "Tricknology"(Revelations 2:9, 3:9). Imposter gangsters are the real gangsters, not the brothers with the little pop guns. These are Jewish gangsters of black life and soul stealing. Nowadays, they don't have to steal many souls; they just wait for the bootlickers and Oreo cookies in the church to help them. For money, they sell their souls and all holes. However, the original Jews were black.

It's imperative to note that the Jews didn't kill Jesus the Christ and lynch Him; the damn Romans did, and they were all white. Allegedly, with all this white evil, how is white supposed to be pure like they claim? The truth is, evil is pure evil. Many of them have chosen it, which is why they allow the evil wicked gangster music to carry on, because they desire evil blood from the original direct connection to Almighty God Himself so they can hurt God by hurting and murdering, permitting evil music to live out their fantasies in a sick satanic way.

Organ harvesting of "Melaninated black body organs"is big business. But they have polluted the great minds of people, many who were once kings and queens, to things of Satan....

..........ANGELGOONZ..........

THE "HEAVENLY"EVICTION"

Denied the right to ascend, they murder all blacks who resemble God: hair of wool, skin of bronze. Interestingly enough, the original Irish "Oresha" who are "Greek" were the first Gideons in the Caucasus Mountains. K9-White "sulphur" instead of "carbon." They can't get out of the Earth spiritually, so they built the metaverse to own physically because the new promised Earth they cannot own.

So, they reak hell for us poor to feel heavenly on Earth. But they are a smart people who studied us well from the caves with the help of the "Anunnaki" fallen angel. Denied the right to ascend to Heaven, white rule and white power are THE SELF MADE GODS ON EARTH & ANGELS IN HEAVEN questioned " THE OTHER GODS AND CONFERRED WITH ANOTHER But go ask the Egyptians: "THE GODS ASKED "Who is this "grafted devil"? She asked "Enlil," who had heard about the good time the Anunnaki and all the fallen angels were having on Earth with the Earth people.

The angels asked God, the Creator, "Will you create on Earth a devilish, hell-raising, sodom And Gomorrah people? To cause death, rape, robbery, murder, and all manners of evil on Earth?" God responded by saying, "I" know what you know not.".....

According to universal law, the Earth law, what goes around comes around. Whites fear us according to the Emerald Tablets. This galactic law has us in position as custodians of the Earth. When we were conquered in Africa with the" ✝ we were also crossed out in the Americas where many of us were already here way before Columbus. Damn, the coward needed guns; he couldn't fight fair.

So essentially, what we have is a black woman who has been carrying all this hell on her shoulders of "Rape" by whites aided by the Anunnaki, Raping black men in front of the whole village. These were sent by the Queen of England and even here in the Americas. They were usually savage mental patients in prison, released to rape black men. The mightiest of our strong black men they would "Rape in front of the black women and their children" to dehumanize and de-Manhood"him. So Much Pain

All of this is passed down through the black woman to all the black men through the "Mitochondrial DNA of the black woman, along with automatic fear. Along with the "Willie Lynch letters syndrome," all of this because someone wants to play God, be God on Earth over blacks, and all under white supremacy.

America's white gangsters in Hollywood and Washington DC gangsters. Well, if Satan got some gangsters, God got some goonz, Angel-Goonz. We are supposed to, as custodians of the Earth, originally aboriginal, to clean it up. It is, after all, the frequency of the Earth. "Enki" was jealous." Remember a jealous God". Yacub equals Jacob, remember his father. Plus, we never seen a" Dinosaur with balls". So, it's population control to control our numbers, life span cut short from what we used to live—500 to 900 years plus.

But they are playing with science in which they infiltrate to match our genetics but they can't because of their recessive genes. The true secret to our long life before they tampered with us is in the Sumerian Tablets. White supremacy scientists and doctors are constantly in the lab using us as guinea pigs, pork subjects, and projects. Damn it, it's time, God is tired. It's angel Goonz.

By Minister Melvin S. Mahamad

"The Mother Whore," The once great Queen, And Kings Of Africa Right Over Here In These americas And Egypt is in "The United States"adorned and blessed by Almighty God in Heaven, was meant to do the right thing by her slaves, whom she has taken from their own land, right here in America. Many of us blacks were already here way before Christopher Columbus. The great Mother Whore, America, never leaves before robbing the natives of all their valuable natural resources. Everywhere she goes, the pale white horse robs, steals, and destroys. She openly destroys the organic fibre of our lives within God's authenticity of wholesomeness, meaningfulness, and soulfulness.

Because of their continual evil towards us, we must stay devoted to Almighty God in Heaven, not the god of this world. If we examine "their god, Satan", through their devil worship behind the scenes, they have a form of godliness. They take the real God out of school, especially black schools, perhaps realizing they couldn't get a good enough grip on the so-called niggers versus niggas. If they allowed the real God to be present and taught in a godly atmosphere instead of a dead atmosphere, our babies would learn to truly appreciate the blessings of God in Heaven with all His love—true love, which includes loving us with our dirt too, made dirty by our open enemy Satan and his minions.

....THE"BRAIN"WASHING"......

The worst being the "Oreo cookie," who looks like us real "black woke Waking Folks," OUR Wholesomeness, Meaningfulness, and ultimately Our Soulfulness. That one experiences when worshipping God in Heaven and sets ourselves in Heaven at once. By America replacing good with pure evil, they do so by cutting God's original aboriginal people off from their original tongue, God, and religion. They brainwash a mentally dead people into submission with "tricknology," pushing scientific methods and closing off the connection to and from the pineal gland, calcifying God's insight to us. Melanin is the key and direct connectional bloodline to Almighty God Himself, and they know it.

That's why they pushed fluoride toothpaste so hard to our parents to kill the connection to the black babies and gave us crack through our mothers and heroin through our fathers. If the 3-strike law didn't steal their freedom by the tricknology of the enemy to promote modern-day slavery, the 13th Amendment confirms slavery by design, cutting off God's original organic purpose for our lives. It is extremely imperative to note that we had lower-class whites who identify with all the pain and suffering we both go through, black and white, and who try to help us. But just because we have an identifiable connection doesn't mean white privilege doesn't exist. White supremacy dominates blacks every day and hides behind the cross on Sunday. Knowing Full Well The Sabbath Is On Saturday But THEY prefer the Their "SUN"god" However,

The blacks, the Africans, the first creation on Earth—it all started in Africa. The same domination is enacted on whites and does not exclude them from Satan's gangster-ism. All this evil has sparked the ignition of fire in the nostrils of God in Heaven. The NASTY Stench fire of hell is waiting as its Scent drips down from the very nostrils of God. The stench of evil by white government and white supremacy, He smells all the pure hate of Satan's followers and devil worshippers. He tastes the hate. They have hijacked God and His original people Now one may Ask? Why don't God in Heaven Destroy America????? And They Always talking and telling "Blacks to Go Back to Africa" because, THEY KNOW WE WERE ALREADY HERE IN AMERICA God can't destroy the Mother Whore completely the way He desires because we are still here among them. AND THEY AMONG US.... Many desire to be white, coloring their eyes, lips, and hair with dead hair that falls to the ground .....SO FROM "Mother Africa" all the way to the Americas. SATAN HAS HIS GANGSTERS

They have gangsters, so God has and is continuing to raise His angel goons. ANGELGOONZ If Satan got some gangsters of white

Supremacy God Got SOME GOONZ On "Earth"&"OF Heaven Black Ones White Ones Too Who "Don't See Color "They with Us" "They Black Too More Blacker Than Da OREOS" They Just White! On The OUTSIDE" And We That Follow Almighty God In Heaven And Are True Black We Ride Together AS GOONZ FOR ALMIGHTY GOD IN "HEAVEN" "ANGELGOONZ"

What happened is Alot of black people all over the world are struggling to find their identity in the world that is "right" to "them" in terms of being socially accepted even a decent Person so many Try to be As White as they can for Some type of White Privilege/Black Privilege For Exemplifying whiteness. When in reality they are Booty Lickers And Oreo cookies Exemplifying the negative

Powers of wickedness put on them and us by White supremacy Hate each other as well is passed down through the Black Woman To The Black Child By way of the Mitochondrial DNA To the Of spring Of The Black Human Family, to avoid the tremendous evil treatment of White So Called White Christianity Supremacy "White Supremacy with the cross" And the very fear of giving us a religion Of The Cross Of Jesus The Christ" Then Burn Blacks at the Stake At The Cross They set on fire of Jesus Christ" Himself. then force us to believe in it. but this wicked "Defense" Mechanism" to Alienate yourself away from your own "People" Is To Alienate Yourself From Almighty "GOD" Himself "and that's Blasphemy "Body Language" with action "No words "Needed" and Many of our people are poisoned Mentally To a very high level extent because , many have been "Raped here in the Americas "during Slavery who were already here way way way way way before Columbus' "And during the "transatlantic" slave trade those of us that did travel by slave ships but Many of us were already Here. Being bucked "jumped" Right in front of our whole villages. They don't want to talk about that. parents grand parents and great grandparents been treated so dirty and evil that it's all passed down to our off spring. we have been made into a Illiterate Self-hating People by the hands of White evilness everyone wants us to forget the black holocaust. but we say NO

LIKE our Jewish Friends Brothers and sisters of thejewish holocaust we Also Say Never Again Say No To The Jewish holocaust. divided against ourselves and everybody else Benefits of of this Hatred except US. We Die or Become modern day slaves through the modern day prison system with petty Trumped up Laws Fabricated to Promote slavery, and above to all"Satan" is happy because of the "evil" His "white supremacy" GANGSTERS NI GOVERNMENT Created to Exploit The Black Nation On Earth Thats also "why Our Black Babies" Are cursed during birth...Page 6th beat on the" buttock" with pain as a welcoming "Evil"ASS"WHOP-PING"SMACK"ON"OUR"ASSES"A"HATEFUL" Gift into this "World"from a white Racist or Oreo cookie "Doctors"Delivering Our "children" during Birth. evil. we never welcomed our people our babies into the world with "pain" No No No No No We Welcomed Them with Love when they were born hugging singing praising God in Heaven Daddy Dancing A "Praise" worthy "GOD" A Praise worthy Dance To Thank God For A successful Delivery Of A successful Life Sung Spoken into existence. and so Naturally Blacks as Babies Fear Whites al together and don't Know Why. There is and has always been a directive to eliminate "The Black Original People of America "Before They Wake Up And realize There are 2Egypts. and 1is right here in America. now that just went over some of "Yall Head$." They tricked us with the "cross" and they have been crossing us all out ever since. The 1st case ever of Identity Theft is the black Man Woman And Child so since Satan got some Gangsters????

Angel Goonz, Make no mistake about it. It is real clear the real evil power of the true "Gs" of white supremacy: Great Britain, Rome, Europe, with the "rope" for who? These are the white gangsters of the beast with all of "her" hell-raising against blacks. Modern-day lynchings pop up near police stations with "the monkey bars" and local gangsters who own the white supremacy news stations. The police always allegedly label it a suicide by hanging. NO, DAMN IT, they know what's going on. They cover it all up, but God is not mocked. We will soon see who is really cursed.

They will soon all be running, flying to us to save them —people they used to and still hate—the black man, woman, and child. When they keep on destroying the ozone layer with their poisons of death, toxic air pollutions, the sun loves the black man, woman, and child too. We just want the sun to love everybody. But white supremacy is so stupid because of the melanin associated with black people so heavily. You would have to be stupid to believe God hates blacks and we are cursed.

That's stupid. That's hate teaching, curse of pork, bullshit curse of Ham.

They can't survive without us; that's why they're scared to let go. All England and the "Mother Whore" America, an evil mix-up of pure bullshit with a little alkaline water, all endowed to inflict pain, hate, evil, and all kinds of unimaginable tyranny on the black race at all costs with the cross. We can't use their systems to overturn or overthrow their evil. Remember, everything is all by design and well organized. The good thing white people have working for them is built-in solidarity. They learned that in the caves of Europe before being allowed to rule for 6,000 years. This world has not been here 6,000 years as taught by the Christian church in many churches. They have been in the world of power for 6000 years and 500 of it causing HELL.

I could expound, but I'm sick of that sound, and they are mainly also attacking institutions of economical power over the land. The institutions of Hip Hop, B.E.T., and Essence. Launched in May 1970, Essence was a black-owned company and magazine by a black woman. In the year 2000, Time Warner paid to buy and own 49% of Essence Communications Inc., and this is undoubtedly the publishing company that perhaps really did publish Essence. In 2005, Time Inc. agreed to buy the remaining 51%. Oreo-cookies and booty lickerz.

However, many blacks selling out don't want to pass anything down in the form of generational wealth to their own offspring, the black race. They did not already own complete ownership, and they started adding the black woman's lifestyle publication to their magazines division. Vibe was owned by Quincy Jones, a living legend. It has been sold several times since Quincy Jones sold it. Oil sheen products by blacks allegedly stolen. All these things and so much more are stolen behind the scenes.

It's true, whites end up buying all these big black companies continually to own everything black because "black" is a diamond. Rarely do blacks even know about themselves. You can't blame Whites"In"Power"because they know the true value of ownership, the very beauty of ownership. While all this is still going on, blacks still face systemic racism by white government gangsters of the white world. It's still safe to say that being a black business owner in America means enduring relentless racist roadblocks meant to appear "Holy."

They have taken over, and everybody tries to act as if it's all success, but it's hell if you can't live free without the suppression of selling pressure behind the many, many, many blackmailing evils"Secret"Events"These dirty motherfuckers,Are"Doing"without the "U," act like they really came to help us with crocodile smiles on. With the success of Hip Hop given by God to us to awaken the next black messiah to lead the lost, with Farrakhan doing all he can To Teach Exslaves To Go For Self" And,Against the beast to stop the beefs in Hip Hop, created east versus west by the same companies mentioned earlier Allegedly culture is being so exploited behind the scenes as well.

The Book of Revelations makes it clear. The big pale white horse is stealing, robbing, and killing the very culture of Hip Hop because they know the supreme value of it. I'm not talking about money, of course. It's valuable, damn it, but I'm talking about the melanin and black body organ harvesting, even celebrity black body organs. The Bible makes it clear. "Though they tried to cover it up, I know your trials and tribulations, but thou art rich." White supremacy continues turning Hip Hop into a tool of hate, from straight men to hating men. Lying to us and exemplifying all that God got upset and destroyed about Sodom and Gomorrah, everything God in Heaven says don't do, America says do. I have nothing against my homosexual family. I love the homosexual community. I just overstand and understand the overall plot to take us blacks, and all good white people who don't see color, right along with them straight to hell to further exemplify their evil demonic ways. The elite desire their Satanism and white devil worship to see poor whites and blacks kill each other, brainwashing both sides, turning the people dead mentally, physically, and spiritually. These Uncle Tom Oreo cookies robbing the church as well, knowing the full truth or denying it for riches.

My mother always told me selling your soul is like snitching. Never do something somebody thinks is wrong with nobody. Because what's for you ain't for everybody, damn booty lickerz Look, she said." I don't care what you do,Even If Itz Bad In The Eyesight Of Socalled Crime To Survive 3 Strikes Penitentiaries "Chances"PLEASE"DONT"SON"BUT,IF YOU DO SON?"DO IT BY YOURSELF" IF YOU FORCED TO DO WHAT THE ENEMY "CREATED"INTERMS OF Satans Entrapment" Good? Or Bad"Remember"They set All The Traps For All Our Black Men To End Right Back Down South to Become Slaves in Prisons "So Make Sure YouSAID"ID RATHER YOU DO GOOD BE THE BEST AT WHATEVER "YOU"DECIDE TO DO? GOOD OR BAD DO IT By Yourself Take God With You BUT PLEASE SON SHE SAID" make sure it's good, she said. But son, do it good by yourself. Beware, brothers, of "Hollyweird" Hollywood elite. Contrary to their belief of the church, with the help of the cross, they have not only brainwashed us with their religion, tricking us with the cross as they did to our brothers and sisters in Africa, crossing us out ever since. If everything was about the cross, why not exemplify it with laws and implementations of holiness for real?

Because so far, all we've seen and continue to see is Satan's gangsters with the cross of Jesus. And the letter "J" is only 400 years old. How long have we been under their rule in America? Well, God in Heaven told me that Satan got some gangsters that hate good. They hate the resemblance of His black "Jesus"original people, Aboriginal people on Earth, hair of wool, skin of bronze. Satan has some gangsters on Earth who think they can take us and take God and His people. Satan got some gangsters; God got some goonz, angel goonz...

.... Angel GOONZ.....
...STOLEN HISTORY AND ACHIEVEMENTS...
.............ANGELGOONZ.............

I know we built it all. MANY ALMOST ALL INVENTIONS WERE STOLEN FROM BLACK SLAVES EVERYTHING THAT MAKES US GREAT. BUT ENTERING HOLLYWOOD IS WEIRD SATAN GOT SOMEGANGSTERS THE GODS HAVE GOONZ WITH FATHER GOD IN HEAVEN"Angel Goonz."

To believe... I know many of you all think it's "all y'all's the 'woods' in Holly" (Hollywood). No, it belongs to Holly. AND BLACK PEOPLE AND ANYBODY WITH COMMONSENSE SHOULD STAY OUT OF HOLLY'-WOODS"Many are a buffoon to believe otherwise. The white woman is the most protected woman on the face of the Earth, true. But see, they fixed it that way at first in their beginning to rule us here in the Americas and in Africa because they saw and envisioned a world like Yacub (or Jacob in the Bible). So they made her supreme with mammies of Black women breastfeeding their babies with black milk, the importance of melanin enriched in the bodies of Blacks more valuable than platinum. It helps their offspring. We often take for granted the blessings of our bodies from Almighty. White gangsters, Arabs, and all exploit "The Black Holocaust." They all benefit even to this day, but all of this is by design. A drunken man will sober up, but a damned fool will never sober up. He will stay an Oreo cookie and booty licker of the white supremacist and goodie Negro and loves it supremely. Whitey says, "Kill your own, rob your own, steal from your own," and they do it, teaching lies through church, work, and everywhere evil exists to be an Oreo. Disappointment hurts more than pain, but they continue to booty lick and backstab their own.

All of this to get along with evil against their own Black people is all passed down through the "Willie Lynch" letters and all. But as far as Hollywood is concerned, the gangsters over Hollywood control the narrative of portraying Blacks as evil. As a result, that evil is a resemblance of the evil of white supremacy, shining on the Oreo cookies' desire to be "white"—black as the ace of spades and white as clouds on the inside, portraying evil accomplishment instead of holding admirable accomplishment. Why not show all the greatness of the pure truth to our people in Hollywood to inspire our people to be great like we once were?

Anyway, let me ask you, the reader, a question: What do they do to so-called "n*****s" in the woods ? Go ahead, answer, I'll wait... especially with trees. Go ahead, every time. I'll wait. So why not be careful when entering the beast and her "private" parties? Two thing? Black people have grown and,Taught to Fear And,Hate is "TREES"&" WOODS"

But quit being so naive, going to parties in the woods with them people of any race and you're the only Black one there. Because everything goes on in the woods, however, be mindful while in the woods of Holly, being careful not to create an atmosphere for "Satan" to exploit because she is "Satan." They always give us a "Christ-like look" of their liking to "trick" and to follow them seeming holy, appearing holy. Jesus, Jesus, Jesus, Jesus, Jesus, and be a good slave. The Bible says obey the land, not the "Klan."kkk" And so, they have a form of godliness because "destiny leads the willing but drags the unwilling," tricking us was easy, being spiritual people by divine creation. But booty lickers and backstabbers with "Oreo" cookies, if we keep trusting them tricks, we've been betrayed before. Look, if we keep trusting them because they come with and they got the "cross," which they "made," they will betray us again... every time. Everything they say many of us believe in them because we believe in Jesus, but there is no truth in those who implement tricks for us to fail. But we must be wise and not be afraid of moving slow as we watch the Oreos and bootlickers of white supremacy but be afraid of not moving forward at all.

America's white supremacy gangsters—all wars come with the big three: killing, stealing, and destroying— with no legitimacy in the evil form of holiness under the veil of Christ. And the only ones who end up hurt are the Black and white people who stood and stand in solidarity as one. And it's sad because they all fixin' to come running to that which they hate so much because of the direct sunlight, ozone layer, to intermix to survive. Evil, evil.

Evil, Evil, Evil. If they mix with us, it means their race will live, live, live. And they know this, so they aim to kill as many Black people as they can because they have a short time. Their evil will never be allowed to permeate Black Earth people and take over again. These are all boundaries crossed by the white gangsters of white supremacy. As a result, Black people are waking up. Many know this is our original land, stolen like the five-dollar Indians, etc., which is rightfully ours. They have to give it back. They are scared of reparations because the value of American money has none, so they are moving to digital currency to further conceal their hate and distaste for us. They need us.

They want you to believe that all this racist police brutality caught on camera is holy against Blacks. We stress "Cheese Nip" cracker because of the crackling cracker, the crackling of the "whip", "whipping"the Black man, woman, and child physically, mentally, and spiritually, all in the name of Jesus.

Oh well, for y'all, anyway, because they don't really know a damn thing about spirituality. They imitate it only from an evil spectrum in which to evilly classify something or merely suggest that it can be classified in terms of its position on white supremacy, destroying Blacks on a scale.

I'm talking about because, and it might be, you have been brainwashed so much that you wear dead hair on your head, Black but don't want to wear your own eyes, Black as blue with blue eyes they wear. It's crazy; they desire to stay a dead people, programmed and slammed because they want to be KKK. They are the Black K under white gangsters of white power supremacy, Negro Black slave plantation hip-hop slave owners, basketball slave owners, football slave owners, etc., helping to all just get along and get the Black man gone. Well, my dear reader, I say to you from God in Heaven, "If Satan got some gangsters, God got some goonz."

We follow orders from God, with the spiritual realm

helping all His angels on this side of life and the other side of life. We serve God in Heaven.

As the gangsters of the United States of America are steadily trying to quickly fill and build more "prisons" to fill all their prison complexes, the more arrests they make, the more they move up in the wicked ranks. Many of them move illegally, and then many are so upset about mobile phone video recordings because they are now being extremely exposed to the point that they are constantly trying to pass crooked laws to stop the American Black public from recording racist police activity. So that way, when they get caught, all they do is get fired and transferred to another racist department to keep all their slaves in check and future slaves in private prisons. It's a billion-dollar business, a multi-billion-dollar industry so crooked that some states, investors, etc., file laws against them for not locking up more and whatever charges they allegedly make up for not filling their private prisons fast enough.

And once they become detectives in our community, they get lustily greedy on all angles, gritty, gritty, nitty, nitty, gritty to get off into some real evil shit: raping, robbing, dope selling. Personally, I have experienced racist cops since I was 11 year old playing with my little brother Donnelle outside the backyard playing basketball and experiencing four white cops putting guns in my mouth and to my head, even stun-gunning my penis by black officers in Niles, racist Illinois. Now, I won't tell you no lie; I have made unconscious decisions as a child in these streets without supreme love in the household because of the lack of a biological father at home and a stepfather who only hated me because I resembled my father. At least that's how it appeared, But I Love Him Anyways because he was there for Me and, My Family When we Needed A Man Growing Up In The "HENRY HORNER PROJECTS"and I could say more, but this is all a result of the white supremacist gangsters in government aimed to keep the Black family disfunctional. They leave the door open for all this dysfunction to invade our ghetto projects, as we were and many are still "government projects." A special shout-out to the Black man who invented the mobile cell phone, Jesse Eugene Russell. Satan's gangsters in uniform exemplify as angel goons of God in Hell because that's what many of them are. The Black police officers are oreo-cookies and booty-lickers of "White-Crack." They love it; many of them have the nerve to be married to a Black "queen" at home, yet he goes out every day and helps murder his own people and says nothing about it when whitey kills in cold blood because of the code of blue. "MANY OF THEM POSSESS BLUE EYES AND IRONICALLY THEY THEY HAVE THE CODE OF BLUE" "George

Floyd"is a perfect example of white color, and blue is all that matters; the evil recessive color of their eyes resembles the blue sky of heaven they can only imagine because they won't get to see it. Plus, angel goonz are all out here everywhere ready to answer the call of God from the four corners of the earth when the order is given and the trumpet sounds, which are sent by God in Heaven to expose and defeat all the evil tactics and wickedness that are completely against God, which means everything God in Heaven says don't do. America, like Sodom, her sister Gomorrah, especially when it comes to Black people and poor people in general. When they make and you make a claim Jesus is GOD and then exemplify only Satan in all your behaviors, ?????? Heaven knows that's all I need to see"....... to know a devil when I see one...... And,then they tear down everything associated with Blackness is not Godly; that's you erasing a whole nation in the name of Jesus Christ, raping, robbing, teaching everything foul under the sun, throwing rocks, and then pointing and putting your hands in their "pockets" and "point" when you mess up and say look. And all this Jesus taken out of school and His real name is Yeshua, and there is no chalky skin; He has hair of wool, skin of bronze, feet of burnt brass. Nothing about the Lord lacks anything, especially melanin, and we Blacks are full of the same, all the same melanin directly from God Himself, and they hate that.

Albinism is not of God; in fact, it used to be considered evil. So they flipped it; with one drop of Black blood, makes you Black? Being robbed of the complete knowledge of self and being done the worst of the worst, that slavery and death of Satan from Great Britain and Rome and their world, God on Earth, the Pope, with no hope for Blacks but to kiss the feet of the Black African King. God will have mercy on him as He wishes, but for the Pope to exemplify that pure truth concerning the Black man's true worth, to highly exemplify the truth. And as the Chicago Purge Law of January 12023, Satan's gangsters are having their way, but God in Heaven will have the ultimate say to play, and then the goonz of God will come out to play,........ see White supremacy Finally realized that for Them to genetically survive "They have to have FULL CONTROL OVER THE NONE WHITE PEOPLE THIS MY MOTHER ALSO TOLD ME I Believe i Was To Young To Grasp The reality At 11Years Old What She Was Saying Now i Do".....BUT SHE ALSO SAID "DONT"WASTE"TIME HATING White People " i Said Moma I Dont And,Will Never Hate People" She Said"Good Son Because That Gets Us No Where" i "Said"Nowhere "?"Moma"? She Said "Right Because Th I s is CHESS"...NOT"CHECKERS" BUT YOU CAN HATE WHAT THEY DO "I SAID WHY Moma"She Said Because The Evil White supremacy Does "EFFECT YOU AND ALL TRUE BLACKS BUT NOT THE OREO-

COOKIES BUT THEY FEAR THE BLACK MAN MAINLY BECAUSE,THE BLACK MAN HAS THE "SUPREME"POTENTIAL TO WIPEOUT WHITE SUPREMACY CAUSING WHITE SUPREMACY'S COMPLETE " ANNIHILATION "SO All of the hate And Dangerous "Evil"CHAINZ"OF"LOCKS"MANY CHAINZ WITHOUT"KEYS" TO FREE US. THEY BELIEVE HAVE TO CONSTANTLY PLACED ON US .AND THE MORE I STUDY SHE WAS RIGHT BECAUSE THEY HATE US SO MUCH THEY USE TO Castrate All Black Men not just to Break us Down To "OUR"KNEEZ" BUT, THEIR MAIN AIM"IS TO COMPLETELY "ANNIHILATE"US WE ARE VEIWED AS NOT JUST A "THREAT"BUT",THEE"THREAT" AND, THATS ALSO WHY PERHAPS NO ONE ELSE WANTS TO HELP US" AND,TO YOU THE READER DONT THINK THAT THE WHOLE WORLD DOESNT SEE WHATS HAPPENING TO US. THEY DO THATZ WHY GOD IS RAISING US WHITE ANGELGOONZ AND OTHERZ TO HELP US AND THE" HONORABLE PRESIDENT PUTIN "...PUTIN IS ONE OF GODS GODLY FEARLESS ANGELGOONZ...And, So white as Far As White

Supremacy" is deeper than the KKK it's their scheme wayyyyy into the future against God's original people.

They know this is our land. They robbed us with the Jesus that they know, the blond-haired, blue-eyed devil Jesus Christ who beat us and made us slaves. He looks just like them, whipping us in the name of the Cross. All of this, mixed with what's going on now The Popes son is Who That White Jesus is on The Cross leaves no room but room for God in heaven and His heavenly Goonz, with angel Goonz on earth.

"THE"JOURNEY"BACK"IN"
TIME"

As We examine ANGEL-GOONZ

If you go back to the 18th Dynasty, you'll find that as melanin rejuvenates inside all of our bodies, we absorb information from the sun. The sun doesn't have to be physically present for its intended purpose. When you mix all these different rays and spectrums of light coming from our solar systems, our bodies have a similar "mini" solar system orbiting around us. For Black people, who are full of melanin, it's crucial to remain forever aware of this. It could very well be a reason why those in power do all they can to keep us "asleep". Being aware of all the natural energy could awaken us when provoked, almost spiritually, instantly, akin to becoming aroused but in a non-sexual way—a dominant domain of communication with our Creator and Christ, the "Mother of Mother Earth". Many believe Christ is a woman; I won't argue either way, but one thing I do know is, when Christ comes back, don't be surprised if Christ is a so-called "Negro". I wouldn't want to be in white supremacy's shoes when that happens......

Now, back to Angel-Goonz .....ANGELGOONZ Let Go Deeper"SHALL"WE"????? AS WE DREAM—different angles of light through which we believe we travel throughout our dreams as we expand the pineal gland and remain "lucid". It's scary but real; I experience it from time to time. These different angles and lanes provide a whole traffic highway of information, which I believe angels travel all the time to and from heaven and earth, delivering information directly from God. They tap into the physical world using many different avenues to "communicate holistically" with their melaninated family.

While all this is going on with Satan's gangsters of white supremacy—with the Pope as their god—different angles transport rays of information that amplify messages from God Almighty in heaven to us. We should bathe in the sun for "medicine", billions and billions VITIMINS of rays of sunlight ordained for melaninated people of the earth. Then, we hear the messages clearly amidst the muddy waters and the blacks of the muddy mud. They love meaningful mud, wholesome water, and organic sun; it's all we need from God to heal us. With prayer, we act in motion what we prayed for, activating the pineal gland and growing life organically and more abundantly. "With ears to hear" what the spirits have to say...and eyes to see what the spirits reveal the art of life is in our surroundings. Only what the Spirit of God in heaven has to reveal, we indoctrinate ourselves with to cultivate life, being careful what we water our dreams with that transforms into reality—the blessings of God. Stay away from Satan's gangsters of white supremacy, aiming to keep us down. They always set traps, so be aware. Staying obedient to God in heaven ensures our victory, with a 90% chance of going to heaven anyway, giving everything set up to fail by white gangster supremacy laws, ...crookedly aimed to house black slaves in the new slave trade, private prisons, and digital money. As we continue to create heaven on earth for "God in heaven" and our enemies, we "Learn" set ourselves in "Heaven at once", creating heaven on earth for our babies, our future, our God in heaven. The white man is a long-term schemer of the demise of the once great kings and queens of Black royalty, due to all the evil and hell sent forward. The chickens are coming home to roost, which is why they are now calling for all outsiders and immigrants to come in freely. Their time of 6,000 years to rule the darker with evil is up. Before they pay the price, with a fighting chance at humanity, they die of passing the slave trade to the same people and outsiders who helped take Africa and all that were already here in the Americas before Columbus. Since Satan has some gangsters, God Got some "goonz", angel goonz they on their way to hell with the bells ringing angel goonz leading the way for ALMIGHTHY IN HEAVEN

But in the exact same way we receive "rays" from the "sun," each "star" perpetuates itself by sending light constantly to Mother Earth. Those "stars" manifest in the form of human beings, and we call them seeds from the stars. While other races hate to admit it, it is the truth that is very imperative to note: the Earth-born children of the sun are the original people of the Earth—the oldest people, Aboriginal people, Black as muddy mud. Working hand in hand with the melanin enriched deeply in our bodies and souls, we are the most hated by everyone else on the planet because of who we are and all we have endured as a people. Yes, everyone has been a slave, but no other race of people has ever been through every evil under the sun, including the robbing of the knowledge of self. No one wants us to remember it all, our Black Holocaust. Nor do they want us to wake up because this is by far the best generation of Blacks God has ever raised up to fight for our liberation spiritually.

But the enemy wants all in blood from them, killing and murdering us Not just Blacks But everyone That They desire to Rob for Natural resources but, as far as Black People every time they Do for our melaninated body organs, allegedly sold on the white market all over the world. This generation is prepared to fight or die because the church isn't working, and religion is toxic. I know that over at the house under God in heaven, it's not important about a religion with God in heaven, but it is about a supreme relationship with God in heaven. But as we communicate with Mother Nature, they, the enemy, communicate with poisoning the air scientifically, genetically targeting the melaninated family to kill the knowledge of communicating with our Creator and each other by calcifying our pineal gland.

So when they poison the air, food, water, and pills to kill, instead of pills to heal, big white gangsters of white supremacy in governments all over the world have built solidarity. So war is against the original people of the Earth for being too trusting spiritually. So we communicate more and more, as the slaves did and do, through hoodoo and voodoo, holy magic turned into evil, is what white supremacy gangsters in suits calling voodoo and hoodoo "evil"? Because it adequately dominates the evil of our oppressors, past and present.

They don't want you to communicate with your ancestors to find a way to win against the evil that America's white gangsters, who just print money out of thin air, then go and snatch our Black babies off into a war that they have nothing to do with at all, only to come home Black to a country that still calls you "Nigger." Lynching all our babies, Black men, and women across the country, calling it "suicide by rope and tree" behind or in front of Walmarts allegedly.

THE TRUTH OF VOODOO AND HOODOO

So all of this, we need help in understanding, so we consult the ancestors in the spiritual realm for guidance, powerful magic. They don't want you to practice magic? But they sure will let you pay millions in tickets to go to a magic show with a white magician any day. They don't want you to practice magic, but they do. Robbing us of the knowledge of self is the biggest sin of all. Smart can only be done by a devil not of this world, organically. But please, go buy books, search the net, do your own research. However, please know that in voodoo and hoodoo, we only used and communicated with Mother Nature to stay grounded, ground ourselves to the Earth, really the same way as grounding an antenna on a radio or TV in order to obtain a highly magnifying signal for great reception, receptors from God in heaven.

These receptors work hand in hand in the communicating communication with our God in heaven and are against the god of this world and their gangsterism of white supremacy through the very rays of his sunlight. It's important to note that sunlight is medicine, and walking around in the dirt is grounding good medicine for the original melaninated Black people of the Earth—the Black man, woman, and child. We don't need any of the chemicals of Hellmart, Big Pharma, to shorten our lives while they continue to extend theirs off of us, using us as guinea pigs scientifically and genetically until their evil science can come up with a way to match our original life expectancy.

That's right, we as Black people have and are constantly being used and studied, poisoned to see how much we can take. Being the original man, woman, and child from the original Creator, we can stand and take a lot. And they know exactly who we are, and it scares the fuck out of them. If we are allowed to wake up, we could but will turn all this bullshit around. So they do work continuously night and day to master science because science is God in heaven. Because God created it all for the

The good of the Earth, and the god of this White Supremacy Gangstered White Man's World spoken of in the Book of Revelation—the white pale horse—desires to corrupt it all, forgetting his stinky ass kicked out of heaven, losing his soul through Jacob Yacub here on Earth. Entering the woman sexually on Earth with evil intentions of creating a more powerful white nation of evil gangsterism in white supremacy, soulless without remorse. The only hope they have is to mix with us, whom they hate, if they want to survive. But they would rather blow up the whole planet before they return it all back over to the Aboriginals—the Black man, woman, and child. Instead of creating a bigger mess on their way out with all this immigration, giving away everything originally owned by Blacks. This is all ours, and they know it. And galactic galaxy law will not be mocked; it's God's law in heaven.

Everybody has unique psychic abilities as physics is true, but they want to make it evil for us to practice, calling it evil. In fact, scientists and government agencies use psychics to solve crimes all the time; they just don't tell you. In fact, we in the beginning knew how to use all our powers before they corrupted them all through rape, robbing, murder, before all the poisoning scientifically and genetically to keep us down medically. And they tell us what's good for us with their evil studying of our anatomy genetically, killing us. But when we learn, soon, real soon, we learn exactly how to use our melanin, activate the pineal gland. But most of us suppress our own natural psychic; so the only way to reopen it is to start practicing. And upon learning through practice, prayer with action, because once we do this on our own in the dark in threes, exactly how to use it, this promotes divine intervention with willingness to learn from God through the ancestors and directly because the ancestors know this enemy better than they know themselves.

That's why they don't want us communicating with our ancestors, but they communicate with their White Supremacist dark angels all the time through evil magic of the pale white horse. This we must learn how to use and expand the reactivation of the pineal gland using the sun as medicine to activate the melanin. If Satan's got some gangsters, and he does... God has some goonz

—

ANGEL-GOONZ...

You'll find us, the original Aboriginal people of the Earth, using all forms of oracles from Black women using tarot cards, crystal readers, pendulums—all precise training mechanisms training us from God in Heaven with numbers. That's why numerology is so important; the ones we are most drawn to tell us about our God. Natural psychic abilities that we need to enhance, but white supremacy in high places of the white powerful rich are so damn scared and afraid of us waking up our people en masse that they have to start desperately doing something, even legalizing drugs and pills they know scientifically and genetically target Blacks as guinea pigs in high-level experimental experiments on the fully melaninated people to test the limits of their science to extend their lives to immortality.

Meanwhile, all the behind-the-scenes messiness is going on with scientific studies through plasma donation centers mainly full of melaninated donors—white supremacy doctors, scientists, epidemiologists, etc., to experiment on medicine they can make because they need melanin for their offspring to survive. They do everything in their power to eliminate us—a damn shame they're stockpiling melaninated plasma for the ages, so if they manage to get our numbers so low to allow their evil plan of white supremacy to mimic our melanin in some way, they're trying everything.

And all most of us want to do is listen to the devil, his drug gang banging under evil flags of Satan. We think it's good because the government did a really good job ensuring many, damn near all Blacks from my era were fatherless wickedly with their government Negro Project to promote genocide.

They believe using hoodoo and voodoo will open a spiritual portal that will enable us and our ancestors to overthrow them—not with the powers of this world but the power of the supernatural overthrowing white supremacy as all the kings and queens wake up, stop eating to die, talking about it's God's will. White American gangsters in government praise Satan and Willie Lynch; they pray to him and Willie Lynch in all their eyes, holy men who aided them in overthrowing, overtaking Mother Africa. Evil has been really good to the evil people of Satan.

It's very imperative to note that white supremacist gang-sters of the American government and the god of this world, Satan—they love him—then have the nerve to teach us that God so loved the world that he gave his only begotten son of all the hell he raised on it, and many of us believe it because we won't create heaven on earth for ourselves. But we sure will create heaven on earth for Mr. Charlie.

Many have been turned over to a "Reprobated"Mind" and don't even know it; they take kissing Mr. Charlie's ass every day of their lives is the Holy Spirit they receive when Mr. Charlie smacks them on the ass for betraying their own kind. It's sad because they turn into Oreos fast but they're blacker than me and you—their Sambo booty-licking Oreo cookie backstabbers, backdoorers, setting up their own people who become successful or are on the way to becoming successful.

Man oh man, Willie Lynch still working from the grave because they pray to him as well in the world of white gangsterism, white supremacy. Riches and all the glitter Satan provides for sin through illusion, Satan helps his followers gain the whole world of money, fame, murder to love blood because of body organ harvesting. Can't let good body parts go to waste; I'm talking about a nation of kings and queens reduced to sex and things. But if we hold fast, hold on continually to our roots, learn them, practice remaining patient, humble, moving in action on positivity, functioning on high levels of very high frequencies instead of very satanic low vibrational frequencies, which only promote soul stealing and soul selling.

Pendulums, various tarot card mechanisms, are only meant to access our ancestors to help us. Through slavery, we used it, and it helped us. There are many books on the matter of which I speak and write here, taught by our oppressors to hate one another by design and has to be filtered out by God Almighty, willingly soul-cleaning rituals through hoodoo and voodoo, communing with the ancestors, being careful in doing so in preparation for God to cleanse us with the guidance of the ancestors on the side of God in Heaven who cannot rest knowing we are still under this hell of white gangsterism, white supremacy.

aim to get rid of the original man from his original God so they can have buck-jumping partners and nigger buddies to hump up and down on in Hell to mimic how they overtook us, dehumanized us, took our manhood in life of the world and hell. We must be careful to be happy every day, thankful every day, be thankful for all that we do have as a people working and praying to God in Heaven as we work with motion with Mother Nature with the universe to put out good energy. "He who has nothing is happy with what he has," but "he who has everything is happy with nothing," so be thankful and don't sell our souls for this glitter and play.

Cleaning out our filters, our organisms do function at a very high level than our oppressors, and we are able to facilitate a stronger magnetic-electromagnetic field which causes a denser aura, which allows us to become and remain much more. Overall, not endowed with ADHD, which they allegedly give to promote dumbness of the masses of our people, the messiahs through the melaninated babies and the offspring. Then they say the black babies are sick, can't be still, so they make you so happy with a check and a pilled-up baby dope fiend way before they're old enough to think, stopping full awakening potential of a whole black race.

They're poisoning us by zip code allegedly—water, food, air—they don't want us to have nothing, yet we invented everything damn near. I mean, every time you walk in a door of a store, home, etc., look at everything in that place. Nine times out of ten, everything was invented by a black man. They aim to erase all of any good we have done, but we can turn it around, even conjuring with metaphysics to overcome a lot of this mess.

Because hoodoo and voodoo are our Native American metaphysics, all connected to Africa, Kemet, Sumeria. These sciences and dominations, Wicca, all through the Panamanian of the Christian, it is believed all parts of the ancient arts, and when we grow and learn on our own research, reading in groups together, loving each other, and we become astute in one of them, let's say Hermeticism, we become required to study them all as we can, doing what the Creator told us to do in love and honor of Him who created us. He said, "Seek knowledge" (1 Samuel 2:3). Please stay grounded in and on God in Heaven, stay focused because they don't want you to have knowledge because they want it all to control you and us all. But not me, not you who are awakening because one thing is for sure: Satan got some gangsters against the aboriginal original people, black as mud and melanin, God in Heaven's people. Satan got some gangsters.

(23) LOOK ANGELZ "Our Natural "Swag," our Nature of tribes. Our Natural "Get Up" and "GOD" Spirituality of a "People" we are, so Punished by The Pale - White Horse for being "Direct" Descendants SOLELY From "GOD" in "Heaven" with a direct "Bloodline" Connection directly to The Creator Himself. As an Enemy of GOD IN HEAVEN, they "Vowed" that the Only Way to Get "Even" with "GOD" in Heaven, where they got kicked out in Their "Eyes," is to commit as Much Evil and Wickedness

against GOD'S people. So "Tricknology" became a new evil religion under the wicked disguise of the cross of Christ to Cross us all out. KKK in Skin Recessiveness and blue recessive eyes are not of GOD Naturally because they lost their Color as soon as they hit Earth as the "Giants" they were, then started intermixing with the daughters of man and woman with the help of the Annunaki Truth does Require Belief. The Annunaki Combined their own blood and DNA with that of a Chimpanzee in order to originally create Slaves for themselves to mine the Gold for them. The Pale White Horse is lazy Physically by Nature; they need slaves who are Melaninated, Highly Melaninated because the sun's Heat was Killing Them of some sorts. Yacub went to work on Earth because when Asked by "GOD" in "Heaven" by the angels in Heaven, "Will you create a race of devils to kill and destroy the original people of the Earth"? In the Quran, The Cow 2:30, and GOD in "Heaven" says, I know what you know Not. What's imperative to Note here is that the simple fact that GOD in The Bible, Romans 1:18-25, "For the wrath of GOD IN HEAVEN is revealed from "Heaven" against all Ungodliness and Unrighteousness of men, who by their unrighteousness suppress the truth. For what can be Known about GOD is plain to Them because God has shown it to them. White supremacy is also Not Natural to or from God in Heaven; it is from and is very Natural in evil only for and from our Oppressors Full of evil made Fair seeming; it was too much good on the Earth so they vowed to stop all this spirituality of the Blacks. As long as they had the animal Chromosome of a Chimpanzee, etc., they were Soulless and so are many of their offspring, it appears. They share evil minds and all manners of evil with the other side of their Dead white supremacist Gangsters in Sheol awaiting the final judgment, helping their Earthly white supremacist in real life cause Hell on Top of Hell as much as they can, constantly sharing all evil in mixing it in with their religion. As the saying goes, Birds of a Feather Flock Together. Likewise, they naturally have the mind of Satan, their Father, which is no doubt the Mind of the Booty licker and Oreo-cookies back-stabbers who are the worst of the worst because they sambo-booty-licking of white supremacy believing kissing White supremacy Ass. The extreme joy they feel is Sadly Mistaken for The Holy Spirit, Divine OREO-COOKIEISM. Meanwhile, African People Naturally have the Mind of God in Heaven. Europe, Britain, and all Caucasian people created evil because of their disobedience to God and the Natural order of things of Goodness Created for the Aboriginal Melaninated people of GOD IN HEAVEN. However, many whites are waking up because of the melanin, and they all are not evil because of the inter-mixing with the original black man. They gain insight through the Melanin and want to do good, but for many, White Privilege is too much a Blessing, even if it's an evil blessing, it's too good on Earth for some whites to pass up. Some people like things a certain way, all and much of this stems from the British aver throwing Africa as well. So good or evil, some people love making evil Fair Seeming. White supremacy loves being on top and keeping the original Kings and Queens GOD'S People on the bottom. But as it is written, GOD IN HEAVEN says He will make the Tail the Head, and they have been on top for 60,000 years and 500 of it raising hell in their last days because we ain't going Nowhere of this Earth, and they know that's why they are desperately trying to get the fuck up out of here going to space as far away from the Earth as they can to get back into Heaven one way or the other even to finish the war to get back in but to no avail, they close anyway so they made the Metaverse and stole the Invention of the microchip and computer invention of the black man to build this Metaverse because it's the only world they will have some form of control since time is of the essence.

Tricknology

To kill and destroy all good black and white people who work together. They don't like to see that, so the rich elite call us all "niggers" and work effortlessly to destroy us and all the good that God in Heaven desires for us. The genuinely good in heart know this, and God knows this for us to strive and thrive.

Their god is Satan/Santa. Money, money, money, money over life is not right. Population control is not right, and in the end, Satan loses. So, the pale horse is also adopting other races to help assist him because his numbers are declining. Asians, who by the way helped take Egypt with the help of the British, are allowing all immigrants to come in and benefit from the Black Holocaust and continue to steal our land.

S.A.N.T.A.=$ S.A.T.A.N.

They made us slaves, knocked us over the head, put us to sleep, and made up slave boats. This is why we can't find many, as they would "love to cherish," seeing how they love evil trophies of death and destruction. They have made everyone join them in taking over the original people of God in Heaven, Mother Africa's African descent, and the Chinese too. They are all in America where many of us were already long before Columbus ever arrived in the Americas.

We are the original navigators of the seas and inventors of the GPS (Global Positioning System). Even Arabs, every race I know, have been made to hate us through white gangsterism and white supremacy, and they protect Asians but not us. See how this works? They are all in love with white supremacy, and many also want to be white, just like the Oreo cookie. They all don't like us blacks; they only love our melaninated parts and organs. They also love our natural resources here in America and in Mother Africa.

That's why they have all their asses there in Mother Africa and America to kill two birds with one stone under white supremacy. But the cultural thing of our natural tribes or individualism, cultural festivals are very important to us, like Mardi Gras in New Orleans, voodoo and hoodoo are all in it with the ancestors. We have the same festivals in South America and everywhere because we are the real aboriginals of the earth, directly from Him in Heaven all across the world.

So much so that if you try to take it completely away from us blacks, there will be total unrest. Crip walking, GD walking, dancing, pitchfork rituals made fair-seeming in the form of hood love. But the pitchfork is of the devil, and so is killing one another because we develop a false sense of manhood because we were buck jumped and robbed of our manhood and religion of God.

So many, on top of that, were robbed of the complete knowledge of self. It's a hell of a thing, and everybody talks about it was a long time ago, "get over it." But we can't get over it ever because the pain of it all is so painful, cruel, evil, and unforgettable by way of the gods and Mother Nature passed down through mitochondrial DNA from the black woman to the offspring, the black child.

So, galactic law will win, but crip walking and all is a unique way of conjuring in California, Chicago, Detroit. We got the ballrooms in Chicago, call it "stepping." So, what we have is all these cultures linked through dance and music, which is highly influential in hip-hop, which functions on very low vibrational frequencies by the design of evil, fair-seeming to a highly spiritual black people who have been robbed completely of the knowl-edge of self. So they believe and follow almost anything, mistaking white privilege and ass-kissing for money as the Holy Spirit, damn. Through holy dance, we turn all negative energy into positivity, but when white supremacy gangsterism gets involved, to hellish ways we go.

So we seek always desperately guidance from "GOD" in Heaven, solely and solely for His glory, "HOLY" GLORY, not American glory, not the imitation glory from our open enemies, the ones that don't like us naturally. The real authentic African brothers, the Oreo cookies, don't like us because we stand on GOD'S BUSINESS OF RIGHTEOUSNESS to the best of our abilities. The booty lickers, backstabbers, and Oreo cookies are more of our enemies with evil because they have "crab in the bucket syndrome," they infiltrate us for Satan's American and white supremacist gangsterism all over the world. So for that, since Satan's got some gangsters, "GOD IN HEAVEN" GOT SOME GOONZ, "ANGEL-GOONZ."

Furthermore, as we move forward with our Creator forever in mind, body, and soul, communicating always, plugged into doing the right thing not just because it's something to do, but doing the right thing because it's the exact thing to do spiritually. And most of all, Black people are some of the most spiritual people on Earth, the most spiritual period, hands down.

Most people of white supremacy and Satan's gangsterism in politics and religion don't care about Heavenly GOD IN HEAVEN spirituality. They have their own spirituality, and it's the love of money and slaves. God in Heaven is sick of all this mess, so He has reactivated and rebirthed His "ANGEL-GOONZ.'" Leave God's people alone" in all your negative light of evil capitalism: upper, middle, lower, top, middle, bottom. There are literally different levels to this hate that lead to reprobation, and a" reprobated mind" is a devil's mind disguised as a Christian.

Like, really, there has to be always one group of people that has to have everything that everybody needs, not wants. In fact, that's the main reason they don't like us because of the wealth of Mother Africa, our true native land. Yes, many of us were already in the Americas, so what? We originally all came from where the first life was formed and made, and that is Africa, Mother Africa, where we evolved and eventually migrated and began navigating to the Americas way before Columbus.

It doesn't matter; we still deserve reparations because we all suffered the same fate of hate from Satan's gangsters. To release our land and our money with extra reparations for the next 25 years until we can wake our people up, retrain our people from the animal America complicity created to rob us of our soul as well. That's also why they are moving more and more towards artificial intelligence to replace human slaves, and they still desire more wealth even though they are all richer than shit.

They are after all the resources; that's why they're in China right now, stealing, robbing Africans, beating Africans, acting like they are there to help. I'm talking everybody from Chinese to Arabs, all of that is Africa. They're all Satan's gangsters who just robbed us and took it, talking about they're helping us. Nah, they're helping themselves when all they have to do is be real Buddhas and Christians and loan us the money to mine our own gold on our own damn land. As rich as Africa is, they know we will pay them back with interest. But no, Satan's gangsters don't want that; they exchange those things for labor equity, sweat, and melaninated black body parts.

Melaninated organ harvesting is big business all over the world. But don't nobody want me to talk about that, but how can I not? When they are steady finding melaninated black bodies popping up everywhere without any organs, and they cover it up. Color really doesn't matter because there are so many black and white people waking up that the only color that matters truly is equity, sweat, and Oreo cookies and hoes in the form of Satan's gangsters in religion disguised with the cross. Now, y'all be good rich niggers and sand niggers, poor white niggers, cheap labor. This is how you force people and...

Even get no resistance to make "slaves on a modern level to do things no matter what color or how much money they got. They still need people to do things. And so the only time color matters is when modern-day lynchings are still going on. They happen in front of Walmart; we see black judges found lynched all across the country from time to time, even black civilians. Just crazy. They call all or most of the hangings of blacks suicide, but it's all drenched in white supremacy.

Remember, Angel-Goonz, we are living in a Satan's gangsters world where we are miseducated. Go read "The Miseducation of the Negro" by Carter G. Woodson. Moreover, Rockefeller put millions and millions into our educational systems. Why? Ask yourself, Angel-Goonz. And right now, I ask you, the reader, why? Well, I will let him, Mr. Rockefeller, answer your question. He said, and I quote, "I want to make slaves out of people, not thinkers." There is always a reason for everything that they do and a reason for everything, period.

So for that reason, we must not be allowed to fail; failure is not an option. We have to always be a nation of people asking why, why, why, why, why. Question everything five times, damn it, if we have to. And we must stand on GOD'S business, focusing on Angel-Goonz, because "GOD" in Heaven loves Angel-Goonz who will assist the mandatory angelic "Angel-Goonz" on our post, who stay on our post night and day with the Angel-Goonz you see and the Angel-Goonz you don't see, appointed by Almighty GOD in Heaven to protect us.

So we need to stay grounded in and on GOD'S LOVE in Heaven for us on Earth as we work to create a heaven on Earth for ourselves and do the best, the very best. Dr. Claud Anderson is an Angel-Goon and getting the word out to help awaken the lion in Judah that is asleep. The Bible asks, "Who will awaken the sleeping lion?" because the government is not going to help us as blacks do anything but fail in the long run because of" tricknology" set up by Satan's gangsters.

We must understand that as long as we have Oreo cookies who live, love, like, and worship white supremacy, they kill and steal from their own people. They tell everything "wrong"that we are doing right"Our Goalz"? to uplift our community, The Oreo-cookies main "JOB" IS TO STOP US making it hard to follow these backdoor setup artists in hip hop. Knowing God in Heaven is using hip hop as an invention to awaken the sleeping giants, white supremacy has taken full control. There is no promotion of godly hip hop with millions and millions of dollars backing it, only low vibrational, functioning evil music promoting greed and murder. The seed of awakening our people by the masses is stifled......

Rich black people are nothing more than rich Uncle Toms and slave owners, just like black plantation owners back in the day. Oh, y'all didn't know there were black slave owners? Black modern-day KKK. It was and is hard, especially in the trying of the black movements that tried to help blacks understand the true truth of what was going on. The Nation of Islam, the exalted Christ for black people, "The Most Honorable Elijah Muhammad".

It is extremely imperative to note that Christ means "Savior." Yes, God loves us black people so much that He raised up a man who looked like us to help clean up and awaken our people from drunks, pimps, murderers, and evil people that were created by robbing them of the knowledge of self. SEE "WhenYou snatch all the land, all the resources, and you can pretty much get and direct a people any way you want."Call it welfare and have nigger little nigger projects to laugh at as we fight over crumbs. The Most Honorable Elijah Muhammad is spoken of in the Bible; they just tampered with it to hide the truth and made up evil lies concerning his domestic life. I can think of a million...BUT, Many Believe,

IF YOU ARE BLACK GET BACK IF YOU ARE WHITE? YOU ALRIGHT WHITE SUPREMACY.

There are worse things than the lies they made up about The Most Honorable Elijah Muhammad. But, They Run From The Truth Aimmed to Hide The Truth Of How Beastly In Nature They Are Like "BUCK" JUMPING, and the ones that got and get slaughtered are Christian blacks, with the exception of a few whites. Blacks suffer the most every time. Everybody always says color doesn't matter, but the same ones cry like hell when it's their family or loved one. INTRESTINGLY ENOUGH THE GOD THEY GAVE US FORCED ON US DID MORE KILLING IN THEIR BIBLE THAN ANYONE ON EARTH ALLEDGELY BUT,TRUE GO READ YOUR BIBLE BUT MOVING ALONG

In the 1700s, even the 1600s and 1800s, we can see the power struggle of GOD'S ANGEL-GOONZ versus Satan's gangsters in the U.S. government as well. Even in religion, they lie about Jesus having blond hair and recessive blue eyes, lacking melanin. The "LORD"??? Evil with the cross and a smile. Forget what the Bible says about Jesus: hair of wool, skin of bronze, feet of burnt brass—a black man. They hate us because of it, and that's the real hate that they produce and continue to exemplify daily, especially in America.

They tell us everything is for the better and blame it on the tea party, but ain't nobody stopping us all from being overtaxed. The 1st constitution, the second constitution is a unified company, Virginia trading, in which they merged to become the interim government of Satan's gangsters.

Thus, GOD IN HEAVEN RAISES AND IS RAISING UP HIS SUPREME ACTIVATION OF "ANGEL-GOONZ."

By MINISTER MELVIN A.P.D.T.A...... LETZ GET INTO THE TRICKZ THEY PLAY "THROWING"ROCKS"&" HIDING THEIR HANDZ"

However, the interim or the United Snakes government "Remember" Mohammad Karzai in Afghanistan. He became the president of Afghanistan; America put him in "power" until they could "elect" an interim government. But, the unique problem with that is the "interim government" doesn't have what we are used to, meaning they don't have open elections. This is why we have an electoral college. They erect and elect that "SHIT" and tear it down as soon as they get ready as Satan's gangsters. "ALL" moral and "GODLY" thankfulness goes out the window because Satan only desires to kill, steal, and destroy. And that's why elections are all screwed up.......THROWING"ROCKS"&"HIDING"THEIR" HANDZ".....

The open elections are only there to provide a false sense of control that you never had in th" first place"1ST Place unless you got it or get it from GOD in Heaven above lower standards. To give those who want to be "lost" and those who are lost—the booty lickers, the backstabbers, the "Oreo-Cookies"—sambo grease licking booty-lickers of "White-Supremacy an illusion that they are good because they are "Oreo-Cookies." And, Chocolate"ice-Cream-Barz" They believe they are better and will no-doubt obtain special treatment over "us," "field-negros," really so-called "negros." But they better not call me anything other than what the "Bible" says God is. And that's hair of "wool," skin of "bronze," feet of "burnt" brass. They better not call me anything but a "BLACK-MAN." AND I AM PROUD"

The Oreo cookies believe they are participating in holiness by helping Satan's gangsters against God's people, white and black. We have Godly people that are more black than black people in terms of really caring and struggling hard because they know the truth or they feel it and they love blacks. They do. And the government and rich white supremacists call them nigger-lovers. But pretty soon all of them haters are going to be running over to the "niggers" just to survive. DAMN, do we want them??????? NOOOOOOO, take y'all ASSES to Hell. HELL, where you love to raise so much Hell on earth? Anyway, you're going right where you Satan gangsters belong.

Yep, brothers and sisters, participating in an unholy illusion is unholy anyway because in the door it's an illusion. Which is Hell-Mart. And by the way, Hell-Mart is only Satan's "glitter" and "play." It's his evil playground and he loves it. It's Satan's religion. And concerning elections, the whole time the white-supremacy of Satan's gangsters already knows before any votes are cast who the electors are and who they are going to vote for because they have to tell them. They know way before anyone else who is going to win.

Good men like JFK didn't stand a good chance because of the evil of Satan's gangsterism endowed in "White Supremacy" under the veil of the "Cross" of Jesus. They have been wiping out everything black and everyone that looks or loves or acts like they love black people ever since. Our votes don't mean shit because they give us the illusion that the "popular vote" secures the electoral college or electoral vote. But the electoral vote has to be in over a month before the popular election, which means these are the real gangsters of Satan. The real gangsters and the so-called black gangsters are nothing but imitators in comparison to Satan's gangsters.

It is all a fraud either way because real Gs form their own Godly government and go to the Godly voting polls like King Solomon, King David, African royalty—a "Holy" government for a "Holy" GOD IN HEAVEN—to vote in their own communities to help aid and assist our people like the true Black Panthers did. The real gangsters are in government, white government, and they normally keep one Oreo-cookie around to make the illusion look good like glitter and play. To play and fools like to be played with and Oreo-cookied. And so, for that very reason, God is constantly raising up "ANGEL-GOONZ" to assist his "earthly" ANGEL-GOON.Z .... .To assist His heavenly ANGEL-GOONZ from "Heaven," to assist altogether, to work hand in hand with those ANGEL-GOONZ on the "wheels of the Supreme MOTHER-SHIP," the biggest wheel of them all.

The wheel in the sky shall not think me crazy, whatever. GOD ready, you believe and read the book of Ezekiel...... SANAN GOT SOME GANGSTERS AND SO GOD HAS SOME GOONZ.....coming from the Minister-Melvin A.P.D.T.A.

Take a deep breath and take "Trump." He comes into office unaware of government or politics; he didn't even expect to win. So, when he did win, all of the "white supremacy" inside of his pores came out concerning

"Africa," calling it a "SHIT HOLE." The only thing I like about Trump, I have to acknowledge, is he "speaks" his mind. Always. And he lets you know he's pro-white and doesn't "hide" it like "hypocrites" behind the cross, appearing holy. And that's right, I said "appearing." You know, we blacks are so "creative," and that's not the only reason they want us around though. They need us around for our "melanin" so that their magic in science can catch up or "matchmake" INMATATE MELANIN artificial "melanin."

But, back to Trump. He gets into office and immediately starts dismantling everything meant for the good of blacks BUT,TRUMP"SOME"SAY"&"BELIEVE IS GOOD BECAUSE HE FREED ALOT OF BLACK RAPPERS FROM PRISON BUT WHY NOT FREE LARRY HOOVER ?????? HOOVER HAS CHANGED AND GOD OPENED HIS EYEZ AND THE WICKEDNESS OF HATE OF BLACK UNITY SCARES TRUE WHITE SUPREMACY"HOOVER"COULD"DO ALOT OF GOOD BUT, TRUMP HAD TO PLAY HIS "RACES"CARDS" AND DO WHAT PLEASES THE SHADOW GOVERN-MENT THAT SELECTED HIM"ALLEDEGLY" OVER LOOKING THE GOOD THAT COULD HELP US IS OUR PEOPLE THAT KNOW US AND NOT THE ONES THAT IMMATATE US SO SATAN I REMEMBER SEEING MEXICANS LATINOS BEING PULLED OVER BY POLICE AND EXTRADITED BACK TO MEXICO

BUT NOW HES OUT OF OFFICE AND BIDEN LETTING EVERYBODY COME INTO AMERICS WOW I LIKE TRUMP BECAUSE HE SPEAKS HIS MIND TO THE FULLEST BUT ALL THAT and Mexicans and "destroying all good for SATANS evil plan which solely "resembles" and "represents" wickedness endowed in white supremacy. If Africa is such a "shit-hole," why are all you whites, Asians, and all who don't like us from Africa got y'all asses over in that "shit-hole," robbing, raping her? "Mother Africa" of all her natural resources: gold, platinum, diamonds, everything. All of Trump's white power supremacy with Oreo-cookies was exemplified on January 6, 2021, during the insurrection.

All this evil is mixed with the likes of a racist, allegedly Ronald Reagan, who started the crack epidemic, the evil 3-strike law, and Reagan's campaign manager. He loved the hell out of him because there wasn't any "heaven" in him at all to begin with. White supremacy creates tyranny for the black race and robs us of the knowledge of self. This is the very reason blacks have self-hate. You can knock a man over the top of his head and tell him he's a "janitor," and he will start believing all he is good for is janitorial type business, being a slave. Yeah, call it "servitude," Bitch..Bitch—it's slavery."EXCUSE"MY LANGUAGE ...ALLEDGELY

Bush tried to have his son John Hinckley "murdered," allegedly. So, when Trump finally discovered what was taking place in the political "clique" and "circus," they knew that allegedly John Hinckley is George Bush's "illegitimate" child. Allegedly. But, the regular people don't or didn't understand all this, so they only understand what they have been taught and didn't know all the dirt Trump learned to know. And all of the dirt people knew about Bush, allegedly. So, he was able to figure it out on his own, they say. But my momma always told me no wise king rules without "good counsel," and so they claim Bush was behind the assassination attempt on Reagan.

At that point, Trump did what he had to do to stop the "Illuminati" because George Herbert Bush was allegedly on this side of the ocean of the New World Order of the "Illuminati" of the "Americas." And if you would like to, if you're reading this, you're not too late. You can go Google or research all this information yourself on Bush Senior. He openly tells you of his "THIS" NWO New World Order, and this is why they were trying to come up with "NAFTA"—North, America, Free, Trade, Agreement. But there wasn't any agreement in Africa when they didn't trade anything with us; they only steal, kill, and destroy the people and ROB our natural resources and call it a shit hole......

I mean, everything meaningful, wholesome, and soulful that connects to our spirituality has been taken over with the "evil forcing of religion" of the "cross" of Jesus and the evil misrepresentation of the Bible, rewriting and tampering with spirituality to the point where it is so diluted that they have convinced a sleeping giant of a people to go to sleep as slaves under the cross, creating a heaven on earth for white supremacy and denying the true power of the "real Christ." Replacing it with white supremacy physically and spiritually causes African people in the Americas mainly to think that white is "right." But white is recessive, the complete opposite of the "original" man, the aboriginal man, the first man on earth from "black mud." Go read your Bibles.

So Satan hates us, and with the help of the "Annunaki," the pale white horse rules for 6000 years. He who has eyes to see what the spirits have to show, let him see. And he who has ears to hear what the spirits have to say, let him hear what the spirits have to reveal and say.

.........THE TAKE BACK OF DIGNITY THROUGH THEE ANCESTORS.......

So, we began to take it all back to survive. We took it back with dignity, with "Hoodoo" and "Voodoo." The government banned us from practicing "Hoodoo" and "Voodoo" because these were ways for our ancestors to guide us, slaves and Africans, through all the evil tyranny of white supremacy. Interestingly enough, we must get back to "Satan's gangsters," the main wicked subject at hand.

Amero, which is the North American Monetary Union currency, aims to bring about a "one-world government." That was the ultimate goal under the Illuminati, according to my deep research. When Trump was growing up in New York, through my research, all he was buying were apartments. By all accounts, most millionaires throughout history became so through the agency of real estate. He had to have a meeting with the locals. His main aim was to only make money. In fact, a lot of rappers reference Trump for his so-called "marvelous ability to make money." He told them, "I'm not trying to be a slumlord." That's when many recruited Trump to work for them. But there's only one problem: "Too nice." How are we going to teach him how to be the bad guy?

Which is what a lot of people see most of the time. To still do the dirty work for them, with the help of WWF Vincent McMahon, who, by the way, paid millions and millions of dollars to Trump. Then Trump became the "Apprentice." Oh, oh, oh, wait? Y'all thought that all those people on the show were "Apprentices"? Oh my God in heaven, oh no. Only "Oreo-cookies" and booty lickers believed that mess. But Trump was the "Apprentice" the whole time, honing in on all his skills to get in and find his way to take over, being groomed the whole time one way or the other, being one of Satan's main gangsters on the team with the Oreos for Satan's gangsters of America and many more of the world of white supremacy.

So, Satan has some gangsters. "God in Heaven" has some goons—"Angel-Goonz."

But it is important to "Note" That "All Of The "Chiefs" On The "Land "knew" what was going on...

I Mean they knew "Exactly" what was going on on the "Streets as well" listen the so-called street gang "Leaders" of the streets are more than just "Government "Coerce" Gangsters that the government enabled to entrap them all allegedly they gave gang leaders thousands and thousands of dollars to "they" say help the black communities but the government didn't adequately provide the money with good intentions because they didn't provide assistance with a true backing to truly help blacks at those times sincerely because the government was too worried about the rise of a "Black"' messiah" J. Edgar Hoover personally ordered the hit on the black Noble Panthers who were 75% women 80% women in total membership.

They pushed the dope themselves into our communities in train boxcars and just left them in the ghetto and planted their "infiltrator" inside black organizations to corrupt the rise and unity of our people in the 60s 70s 80s 90s. Jesse Jackson uncovered a scheme within the government CIA cocaine illegal operating on the distribution of these drugs entering our communities through the government allegedly. So God in heaven saw all this satan gangsters in government were doing to us his "1st "Born" and Saw Of Its Evil And God Raised up HipHop to regain our Stolen Legacies Manhood "Stolen" through "Buck" Jumping" this is where the black runaway slave was raped by seven to 10 white Savages that the queen of England released to conquer Mother Africa and "Mother" America" where "we" "Blacks" Were already here in the Americas way before "Columbus" and once the white pale horses came in the Native American so-called "Indians" left us and joined the white "Pale" horse" 5 Dollar Indians.spoken of in "revelations" and it was so horrible that even after slavery many of the so-called Native Americans 5 Dollar indi Still refuse to let go black "slaves" I bring all that up to show how all this is passed down as hate through the black woman to her offspring through genetically the "Mitochondrial DNA" all of the pain the rapes the buck jumping the pure evilness towards Gods People in the name of Jesus Christ is hypocrisy because they have been claiming to help us and all the while they were setting up the chiefs of the land all the whole time and by the time the chiefs had figured out the whole plot and worked to change after being awakened by Almighty God in heaven the enemy had already passed and made crooked laws to hide them all in the modern-day slavery camps the White and oreo cookie slave masters penitentiary but speaking of trump and others bush were allegedly friends with JFK RJ JFK RJ was also a great friend of "TUPAC" Amaru Shakur and Quincy Jones Now please pay close attention "Q' is a

"Masonic but John RJ is "Q" way in the bayou the blue house not the white house and all this is coming from Almighty God in Heaven and Mother Earth "BIG"MAMA" MOTHER NATURE"MOTHER"EARTH" not the "white house mama" with the swamp in the bayou all of this wickedness in slavery and the urge to modernize it on a very high level From the south to the north so when as many blacks like my grandmother ran fled north to run away from white supremacy all of her babies her offspring were already being plotted upon by Satan's gangsters who went to work on a plan to remake slavery and to get all of her slaves back by way of "crooked laws modern-day prisons are the new save I mean "Slave" quarters and this time ain't no escaping runaway slaves which by the way is more than why the reason they invented the police "allegedly" when you watch "movies" like the "Skeleton" key "you'll see exactly what I am talking about and this is exactly how we know because somebody from the land is making our enemies how we read him by knowing the language of the "Land" because somebody is making all the evil moves in the land and all this is bringing about a conflict of the invaders on the land versus the original people of the land after being knocked out and robbed of the Knowl-edge of self and then being awakened by the Nation of Islam not to convert SOLELYbut to retrain SOULY

Teach, train, and motivate the black man to go for self, the black woman to go for self. The government went to work on an evil "Project" plan to control so-called negros and through tricknology they got them all with what the Quran says is "Simply" Glitter "And" Play "and on a more exceptional level higher than most are not willing to explore we must note that what we are really exemplifying and acknowledge the "GULLAH" WARS" and the black "Seminoles who escaped. and we're still talking about the aboriginal people of the land and Egypt is in America they just played with the books. and we're still talking about the "Mar-a-Lago" which is why Trump is "there" Jackson waged war against them in 1835 and "again this time 1842 they won and forced them out of "Florida" and into Oklahoma the trails of "Tears" the difficult journey the five tribes took during their forced removal Cherokee, Creek, Choctaw, Chickasaw, and the Seminoles usually refer to as the Seminole wars it was the "fiercest" "war" waged by the "United snakes" of America" yes "Snakes" because it takes a snake to rob a whole Nation of the knowledge of self then reduced them to maggots in your sight of that maggot which you help to create grows into a fly and is the 1st eyewitness or finder of the dead and through the knowledge of that "Fly" which used to be a maggot for to laugh at will replace you because everything and everyone is going back into the black man by way of the melanin and the sun is cooking the "Pale" "white" "Horse" and so the pale "White" Horse" is doing all that he can to cook the black man and woman and child by way of Satan's gangsters in white supremacy and as far as the black woman is concerned they have convinced her "she" doesn't need a Black "Man" she only needs "toys" that vibrate and fast-killing food genetically modified to target blacks all African descent in a lab genetically made the same as AIDS.

So when we are talking about the "GULLAH" wars so from every tribe came from every part of the land to Florida to fight the Spanish and that's why we continue to kick their asses they call it the Seminole wars but we consulted the ancestors and we are taught to call them the Gullah wars. "The "Geechee" the descendants of Africa we were enslaved on "rice" during the middle passage the Africans that were forced here to America not the Africans that were already here in the Americas way before Columbus. Because you have to overstand that many of us were already here in the Americas way before Columbus in fact we taught them how to navigate the seas" they don't teach you that in school that "we are the original navigators" indigo and the sea island of the lower Atlantic cotton plantation of lower Atlantic coast. all these different tribes but we all came together to fight as one. "they hate unity among blacks concerning the Seminole wars in order to join you had to become an honorary member until the war is over that's why they are the biggest tribe till this day this very day I might add. spin of tribes are the "crew" the black feet. and all mentioned above are spin-offs of the "GULLAH "TRIBES" from the Seminole wars and those were the names that were given to me to us from the ancestors through hoodoo and voodoo. because remember they didn't let us read at all. how evil They are they "The "pale" White "Horse the masters of "Tricknology" against God's aboriginal people Who Are The Masters" Of "Spirituality" in complete devotion to Almighty God Before being tricked with and by guns" all of this is unraveled and these names were not of our own and wasn't the original names of our African people us. they just renamed us like they renamed every damn thing else after they kill and steal and destroy it to build it rebuild it up to be the pure evil that is being exemplified through their everyday actions as cross toting Satan's gangsters endowed in the pale white horse of white supremacy. so from the names of our African tribes from "Mother""Africa" tall the way to the united snakes of America because we were already here. in the Americas. so Africa had her tribes in "Mother "Africa" and we Africans" Already here in the Americas were already here. now dealing with the 3rd and 4th dimensions you have to overstand that this planet as we know of it because we are constantly learning more everyday is vibrating on and in different dimensions and we have beings that are not allowed to and can not go to heaven nor Ascend into heaven because of all this damn hell they cause us all on earth that god gave us life and a gift that Satan's gangsters of "white supremacy" of The pale white horse revelations 19;11 and so since Satan has some gangsters.... GOD GOT SOME GOONZ."ANGEL- GOONZ"

From "A"To "Z"..... "ANGEL-GOONZ" By Minister Melvin A.P.D.T.A.

To develop a better overstanding of what evil wants us to "understand" is to "overstand" all of Satan's Gangsters of wickedness by looking from on high from a different "perspective" at all times because of the "tricknology" of the Enemies of our creator GOD in Heaven. So we examine his-story when the Europeans came among us we were moving out of homosapien stage and into super sapien stage there were Africa and around the world that had dug deep into the cosmos of "Knowledge" "Cosmic" Knowledge" instructive intuitions "when they "touched the hem of his garment" and that's how we were "Tampered" with and that's also why I love to hear all the black Christians sing because I know it's deeper than words and remedies and so many coming out of the so-called Christian faith not it comes out of hoodoo and it was not the aboriginal people native to the land that caused all this hell on earth. It is the revelations of the Bible the rider of the pale white horse lacking Melanin because Satan's gangsters created race and race wars of white supremacy from everything from lynchings back in the day of old slavery of today modern-day slavery through evil 3 "strike" and tricknology of stock in prisons nothing much has changed we still have lynchings at Walmart CBS news reports on some of it.

But back to hoodoo it is our ancestor inside of us coming out of the human being inside of us because "Good" white "People" and "Good" Black "People Can and do co-exist and have families together but white supremacy in high places don't like that. Because they want an all-white planet but it is impossible because no one can legislate love people have that right to love who they want so please get over it you satan Gangsters'. But as black people were ever to wake up "truly" wake up? and "discover" who we really are????? AHHHHHH "GAME-OVER" and they know it but of course we're talking about "Deep" Deep Deep "African" intuition and senses we know The "enemy" limits us to only 5 "senses" but we have More> because it's all part of the enemies "Tric-knologies" to keep us only thinking in a "Physical" sense instead of the "spiritual" and "dimensional". And the only color that matters to God In Heaven Is The True color of the "Heart" but it does contain good and evil and Satan's gangsters of white supremacy and why I stress "white Supremacy"???? because they took down and erased everything black African greatness erased our whole history "painted" Jesus The Brother Lord and Savior White" with everything that was originally black they killed stole and destroyed and went against GOD In Heaven when they started adding to and rewriting the bible and taking out true "scripture is only a devil and a Gangster of "White supremacy" olive people don't have hair of wool and feet of burnt brass nor fire in their eyes because of The worst Slavery ever in his-story if the truth hurts "stick" your finger up your Booty you booty lickers and back stabbers Of God In Heaven Remember Satan has some Gangsters GOD GOT Some GOONZ. "ANGELGOONZ" although I say and I keep taking us back to the Motherland in Africa it's because it is there where the 1st Life began and you must not continue to believe what they put on TV depicting us as nothing who came from nothing and the white man is Jesus Christ and only white power is god. But it is god god of the world their god "Satan" and the reality is they all run from the truth and hide it from us but preach it will set us free?.....

Although I say Africa was only one race why is that important??? It's important because "Human" race was conceived and...

Born, natured, and sustained, universal, educated, and Technologized all in Mother Africa, and it's also imperative to note that they are causing all the hell they can and they calling heaven have been here Africans millions of years and oreo-cookies 'Are And Have Been" Reprobated" with a "Reprobated" "Mind" by God "in" Heaven" he has sealed up their hearts and sealed up their ears and sealed up their eyes and opened and sealed a straight path to Hell for the followers of the riders of the "Pale horse".

Europeans are only 10,000 years old and approximately 6000 years to rule and that time is up according to scripture and if we use come on... "Common-sense" they're not producing anymore so now they're concerned with "population control" so looking from a different perspective we are really dealing with a truthfully concept of "before the "beginning" so time as we know it began before it begun just like us everyone of us were in the cosmos "cosmic" Existence of the universe it just took our parents some time to conquer that part of energy "Melanin" can't be destroyed so it goes somewhere else it is just turned into a different "Form" we have growth and death at the doorway of the afterlife we have always been around just death is another "doorway" to the afterlife for us all however, in the "western" world "Death" Is a Real thing because they were not focusing all the time. But they are focusing like me love the wool of life for after heart the color of true love is exemplified through the heart and god in heaven judges only the heart remember the heart is "Pure" Good" Or "Evil" so whatever even trump is doing? God in Heaven Sees And Knows Whether his heart is good or evil" but "Thomas" "Jefferson" Said and I quote "for the selfish "spirit" there is no homeland" no feelings" No "Principles" only Profit plus the Rockerfellers funded the negro school educational system full of lies no truths so they trick they own too with the lies sad furthermore moving along they did and still do a lot more evil to blacks and poor whites who don't know the truth they experiment on the public day after day right in front of your our faces and behind our backs we don't know everything they are doing in labs concerning all these plasma centers full of melaninated fluids of GOLD. PURE GOLD That's why it's yellow and if it ain't pure gold or more valuable than pure gold? Why they have them every damn where and if Africa was a shit hole like trump said. Then why is everybody there? Stealing????? Every year the government approves Satan's gangsters big pharma medications that kill admittedly hundreds of thousands of people every year so they set aside millions ordered by the same government to set aside billions because of wrongful death suits. But it looks like population "Control' on a very High White "Level" make laws to protect the Asians "No offense" but don't make or pass any laws to protect the blacks." but they call us racist through their tricknology.

And the money oreo-cookies black k members "Blacks" killing "Blacks" which is why they didn't want to go back to the gold standard. Go ask Gaddafi oh that's right allegedly that's why he was killed...all of America's enemies use to be America's friends" why is that? Whoaaaaaaa tricknology' using blacks the original people of the land is in their eyesight perfect to use as guinea pigs" And you Socalled Negros Have the "Audacity" to love pork. and they target pork genetically.

Allegedly they like the black body Organs because the black body is melaninated "rich" Worth" more than "Platinum:"100 miles of "Allegedly" and paper money is losing its value every day because they don't back it up with nothing but threats ain't no mo gold at Fort Knox. And the all-white supremacy engine of dominance over the earth that God made for peace. Satan has some gangsters "oreo-cookies" Black" kkk" Members and of course white ones like always y'all be careful out there especially the pure at heart. Satan got some gangsters GOD GOT SOME GOONZ. "ANGEL_GOONZ"

...THE ACTS OF"OLD" MEXICO""ANGELGOONZ" THE OLMEC THE TARASCAN EMPIRE IN 1939 MATTHEW STERLING ARRIVED IN VERACRUZ MEXICO FOR A NEW SEASON OF EXCAVATIONS AT A SITE IN TRES CAPOTE ACE STERLING AND HIT PAY DIRT ABOUT A RECENTLY IDENTIFIED CIVILIZATION IN MEXICO "THE"OLMEC"TRIBE" SO MEXICO HAS SOME SECRETS AND MEXICO KNOWS THE TRUTH ABOUT WHO WE ARE AWSWELL.....

As we dig and dig and explore the truth, as we look into who we really are as people, truly we must teach and explore the truth of everything involving us as blacks as well because we have been lied to all our lives by lying people who told and forced us into their religion of SO" CALLED "Love." But the only love we got in return for "our" "Love" and "Loyalty" in all of our "contributions" and "inventions," all stolen, our loyalty stolen, trampled upon. All we got is the love of "Hate" that they "Produced" and then they said, "pick yourself up by your bootstraps." Wait, we are the ones who invented the damn shoe and boot to "Run" away from you "Mohos."

But in 131 AD it is very "Imperative" to note that "Thousands" of "years after the "Olmec arrived, the "Mandikan" "Muslim" Abubakari sailed 2000 ships from Mali, West Africa, and today it is said and believed "numbering about 1 million in numbers today. But from Mali, they sailed West Africa in the Atlantic, headed west, and they left many, many signs on the rocks there as well as on the river "mouths" warning followers of many dangers of friendly "natives." And all of this is documented in literature by Dr. David Imhotep.

It is extremely important to never view our past, his-story, through an "Ignorant Lens," a lens of ignorance. Because yes, we were done the complete worst of the worst and are still being done the supreme "worst" of the "Worst." Many things we know that they do to us, and many things we don't know. But they are wondering how we can still be so happy? It is because we made it through it all. We "Survived" with hoodoo and voodoo from the conjuring up of the communication with the ancestors. And it's some "scary Shit" to them because they live in the "Physical" aspect of "domination" at all "Cost," killing men, women, and children to be the boss at all costs, the robbing of natural resources, poisoning the food, the water, the air is all in conjunction with evil "control" over all poor, black, white, whoever.

Because white privilege also has built-in "solidarity," that's right, no matter what, they are going to stick together with the rich especially. But, all we got to do is steadily go to work on a plan because a plan is constantly going to work from the wicked on us. So let's go ahead and get deep into it, from the silver age to the golden age of Angel-Goon. So the silver is to understand what they are actually involved with helter-skelter, and you won't be bamboozled and tricked with "Tricknology." Wickedness controls it all, speakers, even chancellors overseas, and they all know the shit is about to hit the fan. Because they always alert us with the TV, keeping us glued so that they can tell their vision for how they envision us to continue to control us through false narratives, through codes and spells, words spoken every day, through words they are casted.

All of this evil that the enemy continues to do and allowing other people in the world to come in and benefit off the Black Holocaust, and all of the stinky shit has hit the fan, and the stench of this wickedness has reached the "Nostrils" of "ALMIGHTY GOD" in HEAVEN, and He is not pleased with the smell of it; it lacks Melanin. Most recently in Chicago, they passed the purge law. Yacub (Jacob) in the Bible is partly responsible, and God is asked, "Will you create on earth a group of race of people who will cause all manner of "Hell?" Asked by the "Angels" before releasing ANGEL-GOONZ. And God said, "I Know what You Know NOT." And all of what we are seeing is just a "microcosm" of what is actually coming and exposes America's evil run against God and all God's people, particularly the Black Race.

Interracial relationships are a threat to white supremacy, but they are stupid if they believe white supremacy can legislate "Love." NOBODY can. The only thing the haters are good at is killing us all with fear because killing is physical, not spiritual, and they live only in the physical, but they want you, us, to deny the "Spirituality of the spiritual realm so they can control with modern-day slavery, fear, and lies. Mexicans Loved Black People But Many Have Been Taught To Hate THE Hate That Has Been Made IN AND To BLACK People Of African Descent. white privilege is To Continue Death in The Black Community

(40)

Death. That's why white police officers often get away with killing and murdering Blacks everyday, damn near. And we must not forget about the "oreo-cookie Booty-lickers" cops who aim everyday to please their White slave masters. So they are Black "KKK" Members. We have Black Royalty reduced to "Shit" and made to look like shitty do boyz. Satan has some Gangsters. "GOD" GOT SOME "GOONZ" ANGEL-GOONZ. By MINISTER "MELVIN" A. P.D.T.A.

As We continue to examine our own "spirituality" as a people we must over stand that it is extremely

Imperative to note that practicing our own spirituality was forbidden, and Africans were killed for it. So let us not forget the great "spirit of Nzinga," Queen of Angola, "RAINHA-DE-ANGOLA." Nowadays, we have lost our spiritual way. Our Black women are blocking the sun's rays from delivering billions and billions of vitamins from Almighty GOD in Heaven by putting all that "dead" hair from somewhere else, not their own. I don't even believe it's real African human hair from our sisters in Africa. I believe it's synthetic hair with chemicals, genetically modified and manufactured to target the melanin and vitamins that support the spirit of Nzinger is strong and resilient and "yearns" to communicate with the Black woman from the spirit world to the physical world with all the answers on how to defeat our open enemy "Satan" because she has personal experience and she understands them better than they understand themselves. And if you don't believe spirits are real and you don't believe you can "conjure" them up? Just go back and look at it in the Bible when King Saul was chasing David before David became king, King Saul consulted a psychic, and many police agencies consult psychics as well (1 Samuel 28). She who did not lead her "heroic" "army" in person. Greatest forces against the Portuguese from 1583-1663. Warfare was abrasion, and she is "magnificent," a "supreme" African queen we should all look up to because she kept up the good fight. She fought every step of the way against our oppressors to free us, the lost tribes in Angola, and yearned to free us all from slavery from 1583-1663. However, it did end when she passed, and we lost our greatest "daughter" of Africa. It broke my heart when I learned that Queen Nzinga "pleaded" before the Portuguese with her "servants" close by. She was "tired" from all the fighting and exhausted from the journey. The Portuguese wouldn't even give her a seat or chair, so one of her servants standing nearby quickly ran to her aid and kneeled down at her service on his two hands, arms, and feet (not on all fours). He provided a seat for Queen Nzinga as quickly as she summoned him. He came and provided a comfortable, human, loyal, lofty seat for our Queen. I would have run and done the same thing. I would have flown to provide that seat with honor. As she pleaded for them to get the "FUCK" off our "land" and leave Africa alone, only there to enslave and steal our "natural" resources as well as till this very day. Africa is spiritual. You can't have all that gold, platinum, and natural resources from Almighty God in Heaven if he didn't expect us Africans to be wealthy. His first creation on earth. But there were so many "puppets" of white supremacy. Oreo-cookies existed back then, of the Queen of England as well. She was and is guilty, etc., and she was a mess.

Alfonso couldn't even get a decent school built and established himself as the sixth ruler of the Kingdom of Kongo from the Lukeni Kanda dynasty. He ruled in the first half of the 16th century, governing the Kongo Empire from 1509 to late 1542. He was responsible for making it a Christian kingdom, which was used to conquer us and force their religion on us instead of allowing us to continue our own worship through spirituality. Now, let's delve deeper into Queen Nzinga of Matamba in spirit and thank her. It's important to note that Rome also played a major role in conquering us. In fact, Rome is heaven to them allegedly, and the Pope is their god.

This leads us to our next step in research—modern-day. From the silver age to the golden age, the silver age is rediscovering what's been lost and stolen from us, lasting for 432,000 years. Kali Yuga began 5,124 years ago and has 428,876 years left as of 2023 CE. Kali Yuga will end in the year 428,899 CE. Many believe Christ is a woman exiting Kali Yuga.

Right before this age, somebody's job is to figure out who is in charge of this government, which functions under death, stealing, and destruction. We must shut down the cancer of white supremacy with Satan's gangsters. If we don't, this sends a reverse vortex upon energy, and it won't end well.

Or turn out any good for the family line. Charles Manson was commissioned to start the race war, allegedly with the version the enemy gave us—it doesn't add up. He didn't act alone; there were powerful people behind the commissioning. While they have us looking in one direction, they're doing something else in all directions to take us. All-out good black and good white interracial relationships the elite hates, only because they feel like blacks and whites that love each other as they should. We should all be able to love who we want, period.

But since they're so full of hate, it will all go back into where it's supposed to go, which is its natural state and original state. Every time we plant food, we plant it in that good old black mud dirt, which is full of melanin. When growing food in the sun, the sun is shooting billions of vitamins and nutrients. So why hate black people because of our color, when you didn't hate our beautiful black women from breastfeeding your white babies their melaninated milk into their mouths and bellies? The fact of the matter is you need melanin and lots of it to have a successful offspring that is immaculately healthy in males and queen in female statue.

So, Charles Manson found out what they were planning, and he didn't want to be a part of it. So, they called him crazy, but Charles Manson was not crazy or insane; he just wasn't with the n-word KKK shitrace war starting. He just wanted to get high, they say, and start a high movement. The fact is that Charles Manson is the first whistleblower, in which they try to continue to cover up with their Satan gangsterism and overshadow God in heaven and earthly angel-goons. Yep, Satan's got some gangsters—worldly and earthly. No worries, God has some goons—earthly supreme and worldly supreme angel-goons.

The challenging part about all of this is to be free of fear and to live your life moderately in order to enjoy life and to be grateful to God in heaven. Remember, no man is free until he believes in himself. The bitter part about all this hate that white supremacy produces is mixed with sweetness because we've made it through so much evil as a people. Their aim to separate blacks and whites out of fear of losing a white-dominated world has ruled for over 6000 years with evil. Now, the end of 666 and the microchip are in demand, so they're raising all this hell to go digital as well.

White privilege is real, always, but white power of evil is even more sinister because now white supremacy is in an emergency state due to their declining birth rate. All the killings and lynchings we see today, from their rule up to modern-day lynchings, are a last stand against God in heaven to show their complete distaste for God and his firstborn. That's rough because Satan's gangsters are long-term thinkers of pure evil to benefit their god, Satan. Even though we live in a world where death is terrible only if we fear it, white supremacy does not fear death because that's how they achieve conquering us in the motherland, as Queen Nzinga fought and so many of us fought against white supremacy hiding the truth about our revolt, our revolutionary rebellions against what was happening to us and our people. But there were Oreos that sold us into slavery, but we must remember we were already coming over to America hundreds of thousands of years before whites were made or born. Even The New York Times reports that Africans have been here way before Columbus.

All of this white domination, particularly over black Africans, with exemplifications of hate, remember, we are dealing with a long-term schemer, Satan, the complete evil opposite of our Creator. Satan is evil made fair-seeming. Death smiles at us all, and all we can do is smile back, be thankful for each and every day to go to heaven. Our days are all numbered, so praise God in heaven for the sun because the sun blesses us and everything every day.

As hate and evil forever brace towards us, who want to grow love each other no matter what. No matter what people say, black and white are going to solve the problem one way and only one way. They can't win because God in heaven is not mocked. God in heaven is not a loser, and everything is going right back where it came from. Pretty soon, white supremacy will be running over to the African Black man and woman. They already are trying to sneak interracial relations in on TV as they tell us their vision for us. We are bound by the law so that we are supposed to be free. But the only thing free is white supremacy and immigrants. No offense, but they all come here and play stupid as they helped put us in and keep black Africans in our current condition. They're responsible, all played a role in our downfall, and all benefit from the black holocaust. They come here and mistreat our women, move into our communities, and the government gives them money to open these businesses as they mistreat us there. But they make it extremely impossible for us to grow. They give us hell at every turn and chance, but they will soon be running over to what they hate the most, which is probably why they're building up all these plasma centers to supply themselves with stockpiles.

...............THE
MOTHERSHIP.................

AND,THE DEVILZ OF EARTH.........

IF YOU DONT LOVE LIFE THE PROMOTION OF LIFE? AND YOU ONLY PROMOTE DEATH ?YOU MUST BE THE "DAMNED" DEVILZ" DONT HIDE UFOS YOU CANT THEY NEED MELANINATED BODY PARTS

Of "melanin," "Don't" be no damn fool. They know that they are losing the war in their population numbers, so they would rather blow up the whole world. But if they try that? Then all of the ANGEL-GOONZ Spaceship Wheels from the MOTHER SHIP OF GOD IN HEAVEN WILL BECOME "UNCLOAKED" and destroy them all wherever they stand on white supremacy in the twinkling of an eye. And we have to remember the Earth was once part of the moon. By separating it, it became a dead planet still living slightly because if it wasn't, it wouldn't provide "light" constantly, and no one can give you better advice than yourself, purself within the God within the black man is dead like the moon waiting to be awakened. And Satan's gangsters will stop at nothing, and they need melanin to survive, but they didn't care about all that back then. They were too busy hating black people and white people who helped us and wanted to see us free so much that they hired Manson, Charles Manson. He was the first whistleblower of their plans allegedly for a mass race war. Manson was the first one in 1960. He was allegedly a CIA "experiment" where white supremacy, Satan's gangsters, but not like the injection of the Tuskegee Experiments where they injected blacks with syphilis. In the so-called Negro male, it was a study of evil conducted on blacks between 1932 and 1972 in the United States of America by the Centers for Disease Control on God's firstborn. But they were nice to and with Manson. He was the CIA mind control, allegedly of manipulation of groups of people and many, many, many, many, many others we don't know about. Sneaky devils of hell. And they used LSD to mind control through consciousness basic training but instead of using the peyote plant, it is used in mind control and is a psychedelic spineless cactus which contains psychoactive alkaloids, particularly "Mescaline". Peyote is a Spanish word derived from a root the Nahuatl poyotl, meaning "caterpillar" cocoon, from a root peyoti, to "glisten" peyote is "native" to Mexico and southwestern Texas. But nevertheless, gangsters of the United States of America smacked blacks in a major evilistical way the worst of the worst ever done to a people ever in history which is why they all want us to forget everything that happened to us because they all played a major role in our downfall as they all united back then to join forces to take everything Black and keep it as their own it is no wonder all races of the earth desire to keep their foots on the necks to blacks "AFRICANS" is because they guilty too all the way around entrenched in evil Arabs move into our communities Chinese and all are welcome. But they only there to kill steal and destroy the dreams of our youth and enhance the future for their youth and offspring and they know what's happening to us because they're guilty too. And all of this is hell from the British government as well they're guilty too. The only one innocent is the black man and woman who did not sell their soul and are not Oreo cookies that look just like us but are the Black K and it all comes back to the big secret we were already here in the Americas hundreds of thousands of us before Columbus and the white supremacy, Satan's gangsters came with guns. Now some people say gunpowder is a new invention. Yeah, new to Whites they only discovered it the Chinese discovered it in the 9th century before and white supremacy discovered it in the 14th century and they tried to cover that up.

US 172. that the 1st Chinese were "Black" African descent and to prove it studies show Chinese population shows that 97.4% of their genetic makeup is from "AFRICAN" Ancestral "Africans from Africa" with all the rest of the races of earth coming from "Neanderthals and Denisovans" they try and try to deny us our birthrights all of this is Satans "Gangsters" of white "Supremacy" erasing everything Black "Everything that was and is originally Black" to promote white supremacy and their own lies which is ironic because to this very day "White Supremacy" from Americas "Satans gangsters" China" is over in Africa "Stealing" and "Robbing" the African" people of their natural resources under the veil of Christianity and "Buddha" and many others their punishment in part for selling us into slavery many of us on the African continent and us that were already in the Americas fell victim to the cross and they have been "CROSSING" blacks out ever since and our original practice of religion before anything was Islam "Complete Submission" to The Will Of Almighty GOD".... since Satans got some gangsters endowed in "white" Supremacy" to erase our blackness and history". "GOD

GOT SOME GOONZ" "ANGEL- GOONZ'" By Minister "Melvin" A. P.D.T.A.

(43) 46

Meanwhile, not getting too "far" "Away" From" "Manson," remember "white supremacy" is what drove his engine to start the race war because of the rise of a "Black" Messiah. J. Edgar Hoover's racist ass was serious, and since then, ever since then, "Satan's gangsters have been "consistent" behind the scenes and in public through "rogue" ops, rough "cops." Lynchings are up, and hangings are up and "quickly" written off as suicide. And all this activity is happening by the hands of the Oreo and white rogue cops who are not from our very own communities but from suburban areas where they also have white on white crime, but you never hear about it because they all have built-in solidarity as a white 'race." But the Oreo cookies ops and Oreo cookie cop always get "charged" with a crime when caught on camera, just look at the case of "TYRE NICHOLS" out of "Memphis" TN and all across the country, yet they keep on wanting to kill, beat, rob, maim, disregard their own black brothers and sisters instead of becoming one with the community, not murderers of an already dying people every day because of the traps laid out for Africans, illegal laws and scientifically careful experiments to maim us, our "penises," cut off, giving diseases to attack our genitals. How cruel and much do any of you need to be convinced of how evil these people do us and how they cared nothing about us then under white supremacy and they don't care anything about us now unless we're "talking" about "melanin." "Oh," yeah, they love that. And they will be quick to call this racist, but it's not racist. It's "them," Satan's gangsters in these United Snakes of America. And if they say, "Go back to Africa," we ain't going NO DAMN WHERE. THIS IS OUR DAMN "LAND." They "wickedly" kicked us off it, robbed us of it, raped us, men and women and child, and forced us into their made-up white painted Jesus and all this tricknology forced us to worship their race unconsciously. So now all they want to do now is kill all and war with all is the evil pure evil of the riders of the pale "white" horse. Her doom and her fall is inevitable, the Mother whore Babylon. Babylon has fallen and Egypt is in "America" because we are here, Africans. They just played with the Scriptures and made it all fit Satan's "narrative," gangsters of white supremacy, licking with manipulation of order, all the past and ongoing periods, physical and mental enslavement, and whooping, smacking a newborn baby on the ass with pain and inflammation is a terrible way to welcome a beautiful melaninated baby or any baby into the world. It's cruel and evil, unnecessary. The swelling of the pain from the slave masters is wickedly intended to instill fear upon entering into this world of what's to come from them and what to look forward to from them. Also, it throws the spirituality of the child out of whack and out the window. We used to welcome our children into the world with hugs, care, love, concern, singing, praising GOD in heaven. Instead, we are taught hell fresh out of the womb. Damn.

Aside from all of that, with all the evil music permeating the airwaves and being so "satanically" "influential" and with blacks needing to feel manly and accomplished, they run at the opportunity to sell their "souls." They believe in the name of Jesus Christ, the "white" one. And I stress the "white one" because they are the ones that must have thought "white" was important to change Jesus' color from what the Bible says. And the Bible doesn't say NO DAMN THING ABOUT OLIVE.

1 /49 SKINNED PEOPLE" the only thing olive is the one you eat But they Eat "SO CALLED NIGGERS TOO! and educating the mind without educating the Body " is "Stupid And Wickedly "Evil" so I bring you the "REAL" Like It Or Let It "ALONE" and poisoning the food, the water, the desire to please their god satan they been for a long time killing us by Zipcode. When we block our head our dome as the enemy is pushing to keep us all asleep. We close up the connection with the sun which

was made by GOD, not satan. So all vital messages from the creator seem like a spook GOD in the sky because you can't get the real authentic Power of GOD'S MESSAGES because of the blocking of wave caps, dead weave hair... etc. If you have a pan in your house, I stress, rub your hands under water against with your fingers across the pan. The grey and brown stuff is "Residue" "Thus aluminum and "Fluoride because where there's life, there is hope, but satan's gangsters aim to Only cause one thing: "Death." And all of this causes the African body to go into "Protective" "Mode" happiness depends upon "ourselves" Remember that please as a people. All of this consumes the pineal gland with a "satan's Gangster" "Waxing" Substance. However, "Mankind" is always looking, lurking, and "lingering" to mess up something that's already good "Before" they touched it. All of this behind the scene, pissing on us all and telling us it's "Raining" is as Common as White Police Beatings and assassinations of unarmed Black Men. This nasty substance made in a lab like AIDS and Ebola, they say animals borne with bats and non-human primates look nine times out of ten they poisoned the animals from God In Heaven just like they poison the people of God and made up a religion from "HORUS," which is why isis is so important.... It's not by any means what they make it out to be. Remember we are dealing with satan's gangsters. And fluoride is a by-product of

"Aluminum. And waste no time thinking or wondering what a good man or woman should "BE".... The key is to be "Quiet" AND BE "ONE" PERIOD. It all stays in the "Pituitary" Gland because it deals with sex offspring closely. It is truly the "Master Gland" and if left unattended it makes the "SUBJECT" feel susceptible to follow any and all orders no "Matter" what one objects to, he or she simply becomes compliant because they have been cut off from higher "Consciousness" during this evil process. No wonder why they "All" I mean "all" races on the "earth" want us to forget about our "BLACK HOLOCAUST" DAMN WE SPECIAL. And they don't want us to wake up because we will find a way for white and black to love and loosen and "LOSE HATE," but satan's gangsters...

will stop at "Nothing" trying to play "GOD" and mad at us because of our undeniable connection to our creator and the full truth coming out. Don't spoil the blessing by wanting what you don't have and wasting what you do have, please, because we already have everything we need as long as we got "LIFE." The enemy is playing with life on a very high level all the time. Them being the gangsters of satan that they are, they explained all of this to Manson, who was high all the time but too high to figure it all out. So, when he did and he recognized their evil plan, and it wasn't about drugs and partying like "Woodstock," he said awe Nahhhh to causing a race war. By the end of that age, satan's gangsters were ready, and when that failed, they went on into plan B: poisoning us Blacks by ZIP code, food, water, air, as well as chemicals, medications modified scientifically with menthol tobacco products aimed at Blacks only "Allegedly," and it's all coming out. Poor Black, poor Whites, middle class waking up, and they don't want no part of the evilness of white supremacy controlling their lives, and we are rightfully fighting to unite as one. But the enemy wants war, and we aim to please GOD in HEAVEN, and we don't give a damn about the god they call satan or the god they follow. We respect the Pope because he kissed the feet of the black African king recently, trying to let "White" supremacy" know they have lost already. To make matters worse for them, "Whites and Blacks are waking up, and let me tell ya, there's a lot of white people in heaven and going to heaven because GOD LOOKS AT ONE "COLOR": THE "HEART." And what really hurts them is the backing of the "CREATOR" backing the RIGHTEOUS BLACK "MOVEMENTS." "Meaning" THESE MOVES WE'RE MAKING "ARE "MEANT" to be made to ensure our full and complete freedom. But damn Oreo cookies, they infiltrate all of our black movements in hopes of stopping the rise of "a black messiah" because Jesus is BLACK. Black people didn't care what color Jesus was, but somebody did. So now, what do they expect us to do? Stay asleep??? So while they hoped to have a race war started, they went after the Nation of Islam as well and all our organizations. When Manson didn't go through with their plan and it appeared that the only war that was a race war right away was pale-skinned men and women, millionaires and all. And they, the satan's gangsters, saw what was happening: an ARMY OF PALE-SKINNED MEN FIGHTING and dying and going to war with self in the white race. They said hell nahhh because hell is where they are going, and they will already have their hands full with all the hell down there already. So they say "HELL NAHHHH" because they know they ain't going to heaven. But "Manson" wasn't concerned with the Nation of Islam; he only cared about drugs and partying and getting even with them only. They killed Tookie Williams in prison; Arnold Schwarzenegger as governor in California, one of the founders of the land, woke up, and his eyes were opened. It was too late; satan's gangsters had already thought way ahead of the "Kings on the "land" waking up to their evil plan and plot. So they hurry up and fought to get the black man out of the house and off the streets because we were finding, and GOD IN HEAVEN IS AND WILL ALWAYS send a Black Messiah." And this they fear more than the "POPE."

well Satan has some "GANGSTERS"...":GOD'" GOT SOME GOONZ FROM "A"TO"Z" "ANGEL-GOONZ'

.......BY "MINISTER" "MELVIN"A.P.D.T.A.

"ANGEL-GOONZ" BY "MINISTER" MELVIN "A.P.D.T.A." I mean, against all odds we survive as a people, not because of "Luck" but because of GOD IN HEAVEN. However, against us, please never trust a friend who already speaks ill or bad of his friends all the time because "Manson" must have not trusted the government.

After learning of their plans of starting a "Race" war, he realized that he had the same "handlers" from the government. The same government he thought wanted us all to be free was some BS because he had the same handlers as Guyana as "Jim Jones," and it was all MK Ultra mind control to start a race war among the blacks, all African Americans. "Programs" infiltrate to penetrate, sow "dissension," cause internal turmoil, so Manson started building his army and is being taught everything under the "Banner" of "HELTER SKELTER." It is a "Moniker" that is synonymous with what we call "Anarchy," right? And then you have to understand me, dear reader, because they all have an evil book in which they refer to it as an "Anarchy Cookbook." So tell all, this is the teachings and orders. He, Manson, was working in "Cahoots" with the government to spread evil and tyranny. While learning all this crazy Jesus Christ mumbo jumbo, he is teaching all this to his very "Flock." Both of them, Jones and Manson, in the name of Jesus Christ, and we know that was a lie and is a "Lie" straight from the pits of their "HELL" because we get what we put out. What they've been and continue to put out is exemplified every time we look on YouTube and find all the KKK white privilege police officers that are white get better treatment than the black KKK Oreo cookie Ho, I mean "POLICE" officers who beat and murder blacks and real blacks every day while they all swear an oath under Satan to protect and serve. We know it's Satan, their god in hell, by all the hell they cause on Earth. Happiness should be asked of GOD in heaven, not Satan in HELL. And never trust a woman who always says you're right. Only he wasn't doing what they told him to do. Instead, he went to work on another plan because we have to understand that Jim Jones was "MANUFAC-TURING" "MESSIAH TYPES."

It is our belief over here at THE HOUSE UNDER GOD IN HEAVEN, where I am Minister "MINISTER" MELVIN "A.P.D.T.A." and even in the Nation of Islam in America and abroad, the government did all this because they hated "Malcolm X," The Honorable Minister Louis Farrakhan, and Dr. King. They killed him once he found out the truth and then killed "Malcolm X" and quickly blamed it on The Honorable Minister "LOUIS FARRAKHAN." But they went through his teacher, The Most Honorable Elijah Muhammad, as he is rightfully referred to in the Nation Of Islam here in these united "Snakes" of "America." I say "Snake" because you would have to be a "Snake" #1. You break every "Treaty" you make in terms of peace or whatever, even in war. They break them #1.

But this is what these Messiah types are taught, and all this "hypocrisy" causes sane "people" to believe that Christ is a "Woman," and they all know this. Any of y'all don't know that David Koresh doesn't look anything like Christ. He's like them all, a "cult" leader. The real Christ has hair of wool, skin of "Brass," eyes of fiery "Coal," feet "Of "Burnt" Brass." That is a "GOD" in the flesh, a "Black" man, and Satan hates it. We say god in person because "Africans," all Africans, earth started in Africa. Cain, who killed Abel in the Bible? But more importantly, wise people blame themselves; foolish people blame others.

And so they blame us blacks on earth for being in harmony with the Creator, meaning we are more spiritual than they are in their sight, and this is wrong to be hated because you're the first born of GOD IN HEAVEN. What's really worse is nobody else really knows this

"BUT YOU," and the ones that do know this exemplify this "Knowledge" by the way they behave towards all blacks—real blacks, not Oreos—on YouTube video footage. We have to rely on YouTube because we can't trust the "white Illuminati," because we have a "Black Illuminati" as well, and I don't trust them either no more than I trust the other because they're Oreo cookied up, and we already know how they go. So, we don't and can't trust the press, only trust them, the "Press," for "Less" of the real "Truth."

Many believe Christ is the "Queen" of "Heaven" and earth. Educating the mind is not like educating the body but the very soul of GOD IN HEAVEN to dwell, and nothing has changed in heaven or earth since all this mess has happened. The whole time, it has changed nothing in the foundation of the earth and the universe. So, when we awake every day, we should all be thankful and not wasteful because I believe "Being wasteful" is a "Sin" in the "EYESIGHT OF GOD IN HEAVEN," and a blessing for the god of this world. Remember, "BIG" promises fulfill nothing but "STRESS" and is a "SIN" and an evil test.

We are going to change on type people. Change him or her to him the True Christ is only going to be the same every time. And Christ is not going to ever be a "White or black supremacist." By the way, there is and never will be a black supremacist unless we're talking about "Being the FIRST BORN on Earth by The Creator." When Christ comes back and sees all in the "Flesh" again, all that has been done to Her Children... the development of her youth in hip-hop... and all of the people that resemble Christ, having the resemblance of "Hair of wool," what has been done to the skin of "Bronze," eyes of fiery hot coals, feet of burnt "Brass"? Oh, don't worry about being "Black" on that "DAY."As Long As Your Not A Oreo-cookies Booty-licker Be "Happy.".....

Now, a lot of that just went over a lot of y'all heads, "alrighty"then, did it?.....

Now we have to be wiser than the "Booty lickers" and the "Oreo cookies" and stay ready to keep from getting ready in all that we do. Because, they have a white supremacy agenda they aim to put over on us in the form of " been tampered with and robbed and raped as a race completely, and of the "Complete Knowledge" of self. The whole world wants us to forget all that has been done to us, so they rewrite and rewrote our history from "history" to "HIS-STORY" instead of our own. This is also why TV is so important to them because it allows them to use and access the data to "TELL Their VISION" for us. So if you don't run while you're healthy and young, you will run when you're of age. Running to live, exercise, and...

running to do the right thing not because its something to do

But to run and running the name of GOD IN HEAVEN to do the right thing because it's the right thing to do. So, watch out how we are moving out here because being black every day is hard, particularly for a black man, because we never know when or if we leave home if we will return home safely or at all. But everybody wants us to forget about our "BLACK HOLOCAUST"—NO WE WON'T—because we continue to experience all this HELL associated with all that hell in the beginning of slavery with us. It's hard to forget about every kind of hell in the past from our open enemy "Satan," especially when he does it every day. If you want to know the ending of a "thing," just "WATCH" the beginning....

We have to watch out for cheese nips "Cracker." We say "Cracker" because of the crackling of the billy club or cracking up the side of the head for being black, cracked with something by white supremacist cops—white and Oreo—because Oreo cookies are by far the worst. But damn, I thought they all were Christian, "White as Snow." But, nah, they are OREO TOO, always trying to "prove" how white on the inside they are. Damn, that's why I respect real white people like "Trump." They let you know they are white, and at the same time, they try to appear right. But, not that OREO Cookie. He lets you know he's white on the inside and prays to be white on the "OUTSIDE" or act and appear as the "white" KKK to be openly accepted as white. It is evil knowing most of them are "BLACK AS THE ACE OF SPADES." So, be mindful and stay ready for God, stay a GORILLA—a GORILLA FOR GOD IN HEAVEN IN Nature—ready to do what's right. As an ANGEL-GOON, we are ready to answer the "Call" and "Dribble" the ball all the way "Home," remaining loyal to GOD in heaven ONLY. And I'm not talking about the slave master's ball on the "Basketball" court or "Football." They have some good "NEGROS" on their field, but they better stay good niggers and never develop their own football or basketball teams and really bring some positive change to inspire our black youth. Just stay a slave, but a rich slave, and create some rich niggers that are still slaves every day of their lives, and many die broke for the very reason they didn't start or do in the first place when they got in the "door" and start their own SHIT.

These are all Satan's gangsters over these teams in sports and music. Their god is Satan. But back to Manson, he was not going all the way with his government's "gangsterism" over the "Nigger" in his eyesight. All he wanted to create was a following, a cult of high followers, and to be happy. But remember, "happiness" should be asked of GOD FROM GOD IN HEAVEN, NOT FROM THE GOVERNMENT THAT ROBBED THE ORIGINAL

GOVERNMENT OF THEIR OWN, a whole African people.

Many of Manson's followers were not racist; they just wanted to get along, perhaps, and live life high and free. After all, that's why people got high—to feel free. Damn, he took in wanderers as well. They say and claim a powerful "RICH" white man or a government Satan's Gangsters owned allowed Manson to live in his barn. But no one can produce this rich white or government man. Either way, Satan's got some gangsters and GOD'S GOT SOME "GOONZ"

FROM "A" TO "Z." ANGEL-GOONZ by "Minister Melvin A.P.D.T.A."

ANGEL-GOONZ Beginning to end A to Z. ANGEL-GOONZ.

(50)

As many do under spells, we see Manson "understood" enough to understand demonically. As a family, he was, at the time, drawing a following. His handlers sent in a man named Tex to infiltrate, as they did with many organizations, especially extremely good ones like the Panthers, who started the after-school program and lunch program. The government stole it, framed many of them, and many of them were 85% black women. The government hated them because they stuck by their black men for justice, freedom, and equality. Satan's gangsters worked on them as they worked on Manson to start a race war. Tex was the one that told the "girls" that Charles Manson wanted "somebody" dead. At no time in any of their testimony did they say Charles Manson told them or killed anyone. It was all his handlers from the government, allegedly.

So now they list him as racist for their agenda, and the prisons are and have been illegally filled by crooked laws designed to lock up all the intelligent "Kings" on the land who "GOD" has "awakened." It doesn't matter if the kings are from the streets—Moses was from the streets, Jesus was from the streets. God's prophets are from the streets, not clouds, and our Creator will always send a "Messiah" wherever we are. So they went to work on a plan before a plan of God in Heaven goes to work on them. And their biggest engine to play off is "Racism" in #1 White Supremacy and religion. All three wouldn't work without the three white supremacy rules with "Satan" or "Santa"—mix the letters around if you like, play with them if you like, but they mean the same. White supremacy rules, and they both are (1) in all three mentioned above. #2 Racism, to cause wars all over the world, but particularly in "Babylon" America, but truly everywhere the eagle goes, she stays with evil plays and she doesn't leave. #3 Religion, because with religion you control a person's whole life, because they will do absolutely anything for what they believe in, including strapping on bombs and killing people, which is wrong. But so is robbing people of their natural resources.

So while the rich kids are following Manson around, unbeknownst to him, they are turned into killers. Manson has been "backdoored." He never told anybody to kill anybody, but this is how Satan's gangsters in government play ball with "tricknology." Serial killers never told or tell anybody to kill anybody, so they precipitate a reason to invent and lock him up for not starting their race war. They were mad at him, "so pussy." However, now too many black and white people are waking up. Hollywood is too. They have already started putting and endorsing interracial relationships on TV sitcoms and TV series. I mean, everywhere. And where did all this come from? It came from the "Honorable" Elijah Muhammad, who they hated. He said the last trick the "enemy" would use is the "white girl," not cocaine. He used that to turn it into crack and destroy a whole generation. But GOD aims to restore us back to our original state as kings and queens together—black and white kings and queens, no dictator, wicked white Satan's gangsters in government, the mother whore of the United Snakes of America. A snake is sneaky, so watch out. They are "kamikaze"; they might be trying to get us all together to blow up.

everything and every one of us. But if they try that, all of the strange ships and everything that people are being called crazy for up in the sky will "become" uncloaked, and the Mothership of ships will be seen in full view as America falls openly. We, the faithful, will be fine because God is about love, not "Satan's Gangsters." Festering hate towards the darker people, the firstborn of God in heaven, is a death blow straight to Hell, and they know it. So they aim to take as many of us as they can—good black and good white people who want to get along in love without hate. The dark side of evil is getting upset because they can't have an all-white world. They can only "JOB" us. That's right, they can only try us as God in heaven tried Job in the Bible. But all will be returned in full with extras, and we will live in peace. Damn Satan's gangsters. It's so bad that God made hip hop to bring us together in consciousness, not nonsenseness.

Satan's "gangsters" in dark places are powerful, but as Jesus says, they are imposters and are not the original Jews (Revelation 2:9). God ensures us that we are rich. They just stole our land—this is all our land. I know thy trials and tribulations, but thou are rich. God in Heaven goes on to say, "I know the blasphemy of those who claim to be Jews but are not, but are a synagogue of Satan." They are from the synagogue of their father

Satan, who lost his melanin when he was kicked out of heaven.

Satan's gangsters have full power, and in no way is this intended to cause undue heat. I love the Jewish people, but they have to admit the truth. They control the gates of the music industry, and you better not try to distribute it solely yourself; then you'll be in trouble. Ask Irv Gotti, J. Prince, Suge Knight, to name a few. Control your own music, and they will get rid of you somehow because they have replaced God's plan with Satan's plan. In order to make money, you must put on a dress—rappers are putting on dresses now. All this is in the name of Jesus. Whether or not any of us agree with or disagree with Elijah Muhammad, put some respect on the truth. Was he right about damn near everything he said and predicted? Yes, and that's why they are afraid of unity with us. Even though Elijah preached separation, let's be real—they aren't giving us anything. They punked us, and God is punking them every day. It's going to get worse.

Gangster rap is from Satan, not from God in heaven, because it works against the elements of love, peace, truth, freedom, justice, and equality—all are divine attributes of God in Heaven. Cultural vultures are devils too; they have no soul. When Joe gets out and starts killing the same demographics as Manson to build his own white kids to fight their wars, they are doing it with school shootings now—using white kids to carry out race war tactics. But nobody really wanted to go along with this evil propaganda. Charles Manson said his interaction with America's white gangsters of Satan was to form a symbiotic relationship with white America. That way, both of them, all hate of white supremacy, would have something to build off of and grow. The Panthers didn't give a damn about any of that—only truth and upliftment. Satan's gangsters did all they could to get the "manhood" out of the black home and replace the black man with welfare and tricknology to facilitate the Helter Skelter race wars and propaganda that Satan's gangsters of white supremacy wanted Charles to push. All of their white privilege, white community, you still put into place in remembrance of things. And if you can't remember, we will help you remember. Within this timeframe, we had seen the radical left wing.

Had the Weather Underground, a far-left militant organization, in 1969 making alliances with the "Black Liberation Army" who had absorbed the most militant of the "Black Panther Party". And remember, many believe Christ is a woman. Remember "Mother Earth" is a woman, so to speak. And many of the majority of the Panthers were women, holy women. It is imperative to note that it takes a woman to raise a woman and a man to raise a man after being raped, robbed, knocked upside the head so damn many times and running away from the evils of slavery. It is all passed down through the mitochondrial DNA. The black man has run away from his black responsibility and his black woman into the arms of the trap of evil. A white woman in the eyes of the government is wrong in white supremacy and they are going to just have to deal with it because God in Heaven wants peace and we will have it. Though Satan has some gangsters in white supremacy, we can't worry about that. We have to get back to loving each other, black and white, truly, and keep white supremacy out of it because the only ones ever cared about Jesus or God being "white" was white supremacy, and it is evident who the real racists are. And a real racist could never be black because we're born in it.

So Satan's got some gangsters, God's got some goons from A to Z. "Angelgoonz" by Minister Melvin A.P.D.T.A.

ANGEL-GOONZ FROM A"TO"Z

Satans Got Some Gangsters" So "GOD HAS SOME GOONZ" From A"TO"Z "ANGELGOONZ"

By "MINISTER" "MELVIN" A. P.D. TA. .

"Plainly put, they strip away our manhood before the whole world and then say 'Pick yourself up by your bootstraps.' From the old ways of slavery all the way up into modern-day slavery, it's still white supremacy. Everyone wants to ignore it because if they all go against us blacks and roll with white supremacy, they all win. Even the majority of Asians and other races identify as white, changing their names from their original names. And even if they choose to keep their names, they are treated differently because of their race. This is how we, as a nation of people, are looked at by the world. As long as we allow them to continue to tell their vision for us through TV, we learn the way they want us to learn, which is not our natural way.

When we start to wake up like Manson, they give our children legal drugs to calcify the knowledge of the pineal gland, and the adults as well. Every time the antichrist comes, he comes as a man, and so does Christ. That's how we always know. And many assume Christ is a woman. Aren't we all born of both man and woman? Well, it only makes sense that God would have a goddess. That's why we begin to question white supremacy, not because it's hateful, but because it's a real way of life against black people and to turn the whole world against us.

Remember how thoroughly Satan's gangsters in government infiltrated the Panthers and corrupted it? Illegally locking up Panthers and lying on good movements to kill them, all under the banner of government. J. Edgar Hoover was black and a racist, so mad of his blackness he aimed to keep it a secret by fully denouncing Christianity and following Satan into strange rituals, in clothes, female dress, and more. They murdered blacks and Black Panthers who were good and doing good, developing after-school programs that whites were not even concerned about. Whites were only concerned with filling inner-city schools with the slave master's children to educate us so-called 'niggers' with lies about our past. They used #2 pencils with lead to kill something inside us allegedly and all types of traps to further subjugate the black race.

They pushed fluoride toothpaste to target our bodies and the pineal gland, to scientifically and genetically engineer our bodies to fail and to stop us from living longer than them and certainly to stop us from reproducing intelligent babies to help our future growth. This devil is a long-term schemer and thinker of our thoughts. They flip them around and use them against us.

Now, all of the influential leaders in our communities, you know the government COINTELPRO (Counter Intelligence Program) proactive surveillance, and I must say that

Satan's American gangsterism government neutralized our influence in the communities and full-throttle COINTELPRO does whatever it takes to remove our leaders from the god of the streets. Because the government thought the implementation of drugs in our communities, along with leaving train cars full of guns in the communities, 10/20 train cars they would just leave in the ghetto on the train tracks, drugs, cocaine, heroin, pop everything."

And after a while, you know us "Blacks always broke looking for something "Broke" by "Design" because all of this land and everything is legally "OURS" they just took it and enslaved us with guns when whites came. So, we have a government issuing drugs into our communities free for us to sell, and then it's entrapment because "WAIT A MINUTE" Y'ALL GAVE US THE DRUGS"...

And then once the KINGS of the streets on the land realize what was going on, the Satans Gangsters came up with The 3 STRIKES LAW". And all of this was to fulfill Satan's gangsterism PLOT" because those who thought they were the gangsters were nothing but engineered puppets with power now off the streets and caged like an animal "Melanin". And all taking down the BLACK MESSIAH came from the LONG TERM SCHEMERS OF "WHITE SUPREMACY".

Take Hip-hop, it's explosive, it's conscience, and blacks saved MGM STUDIOS "SHAFT" Richard Roundtree" saved them. And look at the thanks Black actors have to accept in return, they must wear a dress to be accepted and Jesus Christ never condoned that. And the Pope invented the "Calendar" and it's fake. All white supremacy instead of being a real Damn Christian and get along and truly love Blacks and give us everything that's ours and what Jesus Christ would give us bDamn to "Give it to us".

Christians though even though "Jesus never said nothing of the sort". When J u s said follow him he simply meant her way, Mother Nature's way of "Righteousness" in doing the right thing not because it's something to do, but because It's the GODLY THING TO DO FROM HEAVEN GOD IN HEAVEN" pissing on black lives "Proving" Black lives don't really "Matter" and telling us it's "Raining".

The killing of David Barksdale, the murder of his right-hand man, to Big Bull to the murder of Mickey Cobras' leaders as well to all the murders of our leaders deemed criminals created by Satan's gangsters made them so-called criminals once they woke up, they were snatched off the streets and crooked Chicago police plays a role in local government corruption on orders from on high from "White supremacy" promoting the beefs and wars on the streets.

And, beefs spill over from the street into "HIP-HOP" by "DESIGN" the list is endless, and they paint the images as if they are cleaning up the streets when in fact they are Satan's gangsters in government causing all the crime in the first place by scheming it all from the beginning to stop the awakening rise of the Black messiah. And in 1989, Jesse Jackson proved CIA involvement in transporting drugs allegedly into the Black communities and like I say the list goes on and on with all this "hypocrisy" they are Satan's devils in white supremacy NOTHING LESS THAN DEVILS" by their "NEFARIOUS" Means exemplifies Satan to the fullest and that's important because that's their god their Christ to THEM.

They prove all this by their actions and we know all about these impostors and we are steadily learning and it's no secret about J. Edgar Hoover cross-dressing that they would let a man like that lead a government office with all that killing of "Blacks" only to stop GOD'S PLANS FOR US TO WAKE UP and all Charles Manson did was "Warn us of their Evil plans because if you have the ability to love? then Love yourself because your babies are watching and they do what they see you do" so when we call him a killer and he never killed anyone we realize Satan planned the whole thing from the

White House all the way to the FBI because the FBI is run by the president and most whites don't believe in GOD in Heaven Especially white supremacy all they believe in is evil patriotism mixed with "Tricknology".

Manson crippled their plans of a race war and we that desire to live in peace with whites and all have to realize that white supremacy doesn't want that but pretty soon their white asses will be running over to us because of the melanin in order for their offspring to survive" but everything is going back into from which ti came satans got some gangsters, God got some goons

"MINISTER"MELVIN"A.P.D.T.A.
..................ANGELGOONZ

ANGEL-GOONZ BY MINISTER MELVIN A.P.D.T.A.

(56)

ANGELGOONZ must beware and pay very close attention. Don't be concerned with what they want us to believe about Manson being crazy and racist. What we need to worry about and focus on is loving ourselves as a people, as a special group despite the evils of the world and their perceptions of us. They have been "Reprobated" by God, following fair-seeming forms of godliness but denying its true power. No political group or politician comes in on a platform of leadership running for office on the grounds of taking care of other people; even other nations love their own people first and put others last. Chinese, Japanese, Russians, Mexicans—everybody loves their own first, and nobody calls them racist. The Jews, I love them, but nobody calls them racist when they love their own and say "NEVER" again to their Holocaust. But as soon as Blacks say "never again" to rape, murder, police assassinations on TV or anywhere, no more robbing us of everything, no more setting us up and putting us in your prisons as slaves (the 13th Amendment creating crooked laws to enslave Blacks), and cover up everything with the "CROSS" of Jesus—all this hypocrisy, claiming to be Christians and treating Blacks like this, is evil, the worst of the worst.

Taking our land from us, we were already here in the Americas, and Satan's gangsters aim to keep lying and telling more lies to keep the world against us because they themselves are against us and are not of the Christ they claim, only the one of white supremacy. Others because the energy then remembers then so-called niggers last. But be what you peni Christian or Buddha, it doesn't matter, just treat Blacks better, but take care of your own first. There is just a strong "National" CONSTRUCT" against us "Blacks" now let's get deep into it.

Oh yes, we are "YES" WE ARE every 10 years they expand in the census all immigrants as minorities; the Chinese came in, got free land, and in 1870 when it broke out there was about 4000 Hispanic in the country straight from Europe and Spain which was after the Civil War broke out and there was none until after, and they even got paid. But everybody we're talking about played a major role in taking "AFRICA" and enslaving us there, and all that was going on over here while everything else was taking place against us here in the Americas where many of us already were. See, we had been coming to the Americas hundreds of thousands of years by sea way before anybody else knew how to navigate the high seas; we were the only navigators. We taught everybody else; they just treat us like shit instead of treating us like Buddha and Jesus and all says treat us which is to treat others like you would have them treat you. Anyway, they were allowed to start businesses, but we worked side by side for free; we worked and for good pay did the Chinese work on the railroads, etc., and the evil continues because students are to be able to go get grants for school, but Blacks can't; it's hard, but poor whites can go to the NAACP college fund and get funds for free college, but Blacks can't. Everybody else can and for free. And we, the real Indians, keep in mind that in 1789, they had only planted one Black federal Oreo cookie judge, and I mean in all the time I have spoken of here, and Dr.

Claude Anderson came in and appointed three. Dr. Claude Anderson is an ANGELGOON from GOD IN HEAVEN. In 1789, the Constitution was drafted; no school will teach this. Two groups, Whites and Black immigrants="Native Blacks", 9% of Blacks in this country are from America. We don't own anything from Africa anymore once we left Africa way before Columbus 1,000s of years. We don't get Christmas Cards from Africa—we had lower class, upper class George Washington, Hamilton, all the founding fathers drafted this scheme to start their democracy and borrowed money from all the banks in Europe, the white ones. George Washington said all the wealth is in the land, so I want 100,000 in acreage. So, they stole our land, enslaved us, and took it. Hamilton did the same; he wanted 100,000 acres of land, and so on. So 50,000 acres here and there, to all except the blacks. Give all land to poor whites from England, Europe, and all over the world come here just like Africa, let's take everything from these nigers here in the Americas too, and they did.

Charles Manson didn't have anything to do with that. They just wanted to keep the hand and to stay. Satan's gangster book the Satans name, it has to be Satans name because Jesus Christ would have nothing to do with this evil, and it's pure hell. The very first case of identity theft is the white supremacy government robbing blacks of the knowledge of self, poisoning everything we have, killing us by zipcode. As black people, we call Manson crazy; I think it's clear who's crazy here. They just wanted to have a reason to lock him up and make a white trash slave out of him for not going through with their plans for a major race war between Blacks and Whites. They got mad when he said the Black man is GOD was GOD and is GOD. When he was in his native land, he was the gorilla, speaking of the Black man being reduced to a thing, knocked upside the head from the Congo, the jungle when the Congo gorilla is the key, the golden key. I'm a gorilla too, brothers and sisters, and an ANGELGOON sent to do GODS WORK, and I will not fail.

So, we must talk and read straight from GOD. It's imperative tonight that it all falls back on the gorilla GOD raises up, no punks, gold key-solar key, and going into the solar into the sun cycle. And the pope built and designed time around the black woman's cycles, nine months, etc. Playing God, the sun, which loves us, by the way of melanin and the pineal gland interactions. But the father's right to rule must be accompanied by what? It must be accompanied by the mother's right to inherit the silver key. We must be positive and straightforward with our community. It's imperative to stay focused and for me to do my best to reach my people no matter what and to educate as many as I can with the truth because the truth doesn't need any help unless it's been tampered with and hidden in all places by white supremacy in darkness. Because whites and blacks that are poor are waking up and want no part in the rich and the powerful wanting race war to shape their rich world to exclude the poor is evil. All knowledge of the original man, the divine black man, and his queen, both once kings and queens now reduced to dust balls at all costs to keep us asleep and to white out everything are Satan's gangsters, but there is a difference between real black men and real black women, many are now Oreo cookies and back-doorers, and they are the Black KKK and we must watch out from them, stay far away from them, because they are converted KKK members and they kill their own and set up their own and nowadays white supremacy is paying Oreo cookies to murder black babies for the melaninated body parts, and they sell black body organs at all costs, kill and steal, and destroy the blacks, kidnap, take, rob black's organs in Chicago, and all across the world is big business and all this mess with cancer and mankind made diseases, Dr. Sebi cured them all, damn near, and they killed him for curing many blacks and whites because he was messing up their plans with Big Pharma, it's big business, and Satan's got some gang-sters, and GOD got some goonz from "A" to "Z," ANGELGOONZ

BY MINISTER"MELVIN"A. P.D.T.A..... "ANGEL-GOONZ". ANGELGOONZ

As we examine all that we can, going deep and deeper into why we are truthfully in this situation as a people, once kings and queens, we must also examine the biological and chemical traps of the implementation of drugs put in our community by the very same government who swear they want to help us. You don't set a people up that you enslaved physically for hundreds and hundreds of years in the name of Jesus Christ, and now, you — white supremacy — aim to control the blacks mentally with drugs so that they have and create an atmosphere for Satan to exploit. We were exploited so they can come in and take our babies and further the rise of a black messiah. I too was a "victim," born addicted; my father was a heroin addict. I was born a premature baby because of all the government drugs imposed in our communities for the white supremacist "PROJECT" that they made to control our narratives and to stop the kings from waking up.

But with exercise, I learned how to use my body and to build mentally within myself. The best place for me to ever go was inside my "SOUL," my very soul, to figure it all out with the help of melanin and focusing in the sun, digging deep to connect with my ancestors and God in heaven. But dealing with and discovering "my" then "our" open enemy, I begin to realize these people can't believe in all the lies that they preach in church about Christ and God. They kill, steal, and destroy all manners of black growth, authenticity, inventions, and all they just steal, kill, and destroy. While people are trying to get their lives together and move on, we have the very same government working to kill and steal everything that they claim they want us to have. It was all a lie, and with millions of drug babies running around sick, not knowing why, poisoning the black babies, experimenting on us left and right. This is deeper than the Tuskegee experiments. I've come to the realization that the only people who are going to help us truly are us, along with all the interracial families. We all have to come together, or they are just going to give all our resources to foreigners and white rich. White supremacy has now aimed to get rid of lower-class whites by making meth, right up under the kitchen sink. What goes around comes around now that which they intended to use natural cocoa plant to make and manufacture cocaine and heroin to take down the black African race has now backfired. No longer is the cocoa plant naturally needed even though they used to put cocaine in Coca-Cola. Now they're using and making meth from household products to get high themselves.

The government made meth allegedly to get rid of all poor, so-called "Nigger Lovers" and white trash, and they're using meth to do it, and nobody's paying attention. But God in Heaven is. You know, hundreds of thousands of us Africans were already here in the Americas and were simply robbed, raped, killed, and forced to fight in wars to further white supremacy. But all this drug mess has me learning the importance of exercising, cleaning the body, prayer, soul-digging, calling out to God out loud. I didn't really know why, and I'm talking all through my twenties, searching why, why, why, why, why, God digging at me constantly, driving me crazy, I thought, but it was God in Heaven trying hard to awaken me as an ANGEL-GOON. The drug from birth and everything else associated with that, I don't expect anyone to fully understand, but as many are taught to "understand," I realize the overall plot and all Manson wanted to do was get high and party, but now they've done. Man made a drug, and God in Heaven is taking them down with it. I see a lot of politicians using meth every day, lawyers, judges, etc., but exercise is a tool I use even to this day with meditation to keep it all together, communicating with my ancestors in spirit, all of them because they have guidance to show if we listen to what the spirits have to say. But they don't want us to listen to those heavenly spirits of truth because the ancestors can guide us best because they know this devil enemy better than they know themselves. So they make drugs and feed us fluoride toothpaste to close up and calcify the pineal gland so that we don't listen to the spirits of truth. You have to overstand that the enemy prays to his ancestors of evil for evil.

Guidance all the time. So God in heaven helps me by revealing the truth in a world white supremacy has designed to lie and adopt what is fair-seeming as truth from God in heaven. When in fact, it's all an illusion straight to hell because all their actions say that's where they know they're going. And if they believed in Jesus Christ, why are they so damn evil in the name of Jesus Christ, taking oaths to uphold God, but which God? And when I realize what all the fuss and all the fight was and is about, I say I got to warn and awaken my people and all who will listen. Being no longer concerned with the glitter and play of this world mixed in with tricknology, we must avoid and also the spirit of Malcolm X is deeply embedded in me to do the right thing and to expose the truth. His spirit is from almighty God in Heaven.

I love Father God in Heaven. I hate Satan and all his minions because all they do is divide and conquer the poor in the name of money and slaves. Then they're closing all the black schools and opening more and more prisons in the name of Jesus Christ and money. But I thought Jesus overturned the money changers for illegal financial gain under white supremacy. But the ability to see through all their tricknology requires a different viewpoint and changing one's perception and we change our lives by looking from a different view-point and we see all the deception and able to under-stand what we need to do to defeat this evil beast who only desires to take as many to hell with himself full of white evil hell, no melanin, just pale, stale hell and raising all hell all the way full of riches in this world gaining the whole world but losing and done lost their souls.

So they want us to lose ours or sell it so they can have hell company and the problem and premise with promise false promises is how they fool fools. We must understand how to adequately protect and correct ourselves, how to go and find out who they are connected to. Half of them take adrenaline chrome is like playing with crack is a trick they use, a drug to get you the promise of drugs and the adrenaline rush through science. They study us and use drugs to control us and then here comes the snitching and prison, all connected, and we have more and more of this cheese nip activity going on. And nobody who needs to be paying attention is paying attention. The world around everyone is going to shit in the name of bullshit to get as many to go to hell with their booty-licking Oreo cookie-ism, backdoorers, backstabbers of your own people, is all by design.

Satan has some gangsters. God got some goonz from "A" to "Z".

ANGELGOONZ BY MINISTER MELVIN A.P.D.T.A. ."ANGEL-GOONZ" ...

FROM "A"TO"Z"— -"ANGELGOONZ"

As we delve deeper into ANGELGOONZ and traverse various timelines, we must not forget the "black codes" and how "Satans" Gangsters administered their hatred towards African people. The pure envy and how they used their hate to express exactly how they felt, and still feel today, in terms of how they controlled and continue to control us to this very day. We're mentally in chains as a whole Black African nation. Originally, women made up the nation of a kingdom and our African kings didn't sit on the throne to command, dictate, demean, or mistreat the people, nor demand wealth. No, we sat on the throne in place of our ancestors, reduced to nothing in their eyes and in the world. We have been coming to the Americas for over 50,000 years.

As for the black codes, they aimed to educate us Blacks, many of whom were already here, on the basis of servants under white supremacy. But a king's responsibility is to sit as the ancestor of ancestors, speaking for them and interpreting their will to the community. However, in Satan's Gangsters' world, things were different. There was a partnership between African kings and powerful women, nothing like the lies we were taught. Even today, we have many female kings in Africa.

To keep things truthful, women hold power in roles in nature, though your sperm fertilizes the egg, it runs deeper than that. When we look at the king, we must not mistake European culture for African culture. We have been robbed of complete knowledge of self and must study and re-educate ourselves with vigor because we have internalized white supremacy. We're not taught of woman kings in Africa, the Americas' control over the original people of the earth, and that all life started in Africa. It's something we Blacks are envied and hated for. They educate us solely on the "basis" of servants. Childlike, many of our ancestors sold us into slavery. But with the "barrel" of a gun by white supremacy, now we have Blacks selling drugs to one another and killing.

Yet, we have to go deep to show where it all stems from: Satans Gangsters with guns. We had no guns. The first time hearing a blast from cannons, etc., etymology, child-rearing, or training of animals is how they, white supremacy, treat us that way to this day, many of us.

In 1825 Webster states "educate" derives from the Latin word to "Lead." "NIGGERS" Like "animals," so to speak. "To instruct as to inform as a child principles of art" 1828 Webster. All this is constant as we see through the black codes the bringing up as a child instructions and disci-pline which is intended to enlighten the understanding correcting the "temperd" and "form" the "manners" and "habits" of the nigger youth and fit them for "usefulness" in the "future" and it all goes back to Willie Lynch letters concepts.

Also, in 1866 to make and enforce contracts to take and to steal land from us who were already here and just took our land called us Indians mixed us all in with each other and called all us niggers contracts evidence to inherit purchase, lease, sell hold convoy real and personal property and to fill and equal "benefit" of all laws and "proceedings for securities of "persons" and "personal" property as enjoyed by white supremacy so openly by white citizens civil rights act 1866 "Satans" "Gangsters" but as a African "People" we don't go through darkness to be in it. We go into the darkness to create the light in which all to see.

All of this taking place as we look at the change in the timeline is so subtle, we were not noticing it, but, it has been shifting in the position of the magnetic pole when it's snowing in the "desert." This is how we know the magnetic field is changing its position in reverse phenomenon to take place snow in Texas deep freezes and also in Arabia in the same shit storm huckle buck. All at the same time that's because the energy on the electricity following the path of resistance electric magnetic field began to move through the earth we're going to be able to see the effects in all of this that is being discussed here in the atmosphere because the atmosphere is affected by the frequency and the vibration of the earth and the energy that white supremacy puts out in the vibrations of the earth. Which is why "oreo" cookies functions so deeply lowly vibrational frequencies and so as the amount of water that evaporates from the oceans sands along with the along with the positioning of under water rivers that many don't believe exists so go there and you can end up in what is called a sinkhole in Michigan and come out ending up in the Pacific Ocean through an underground river they always spring up in the deserts, the grid the shifting of the lies of white supremacy as well does shift with it in all the lies from a Gangsterous government they will tell us that these

(62)

Plates are moving, tectonic plates are moving, but it's not the plates this time; it's the electromagnetic field. We are under what is called an "evil response in the frequency by the Earth to clean it up, and now it's time to flip the degrees in a shoe, a definite resonate. If any of you go to Egyptology, you'll see physics of it all in the hieroglyphics, how it functions and what it does to shift degrees, shifting the grid. This is the electric magnetic pole shift. But before Nibiru would come close enough to cause these tectonic plates to slide into position on the planet. Believe me, this is why they use the South to divide and conquer and as a down phenomenon to twist our brains to believe that the Earth grid had flipped because we are sleeping and sleep Black nation of a people that goes deeper and deeper than the enemy wants us to know, with others working in the wrong orientation and have our visual cortex distorted like some of you all reading this right here right now. It appears distorted because it's the truth far from what you have been taught because the perception is that it resembles GPS. You need three points of conversions and, along with the correct coordinated to know what frequency to navigate, but they won't tell you that you are capable of this when you move into your higher senses and even send and receive text messages with our brains, no device needed, no physical form but with our mind. Melaninated bodies, melaninated brains operate and expand the pineal gland. You are the antibodies to the Earth like your white blood cells are to your bodies, and that's probably why they invented AIDS... just shows you that Satan got some gangsters. God got some goonz from A to Z. ANGELGOONZ.

by Minister Melvin A.P.D. T.A.

"ANGEL"-"GOONZ"....."ANGELGOONZ"

ANGELGOONZ

As Mentioned before concerning white blood cells is vital to life period. inventing aids and other "Pathogens" to genetical!:

created for peace? well to simply answer that question go to the bible

Psalm 106:47 and Deuteronomy 30 speak directly to us, the only nation that fits the criteria as a people where all life began, whom God could be referring to. From the transatlantic slave trade to the conquest of those of us already in the Americas, the Bible makes it clear that we would be scattered to the four corners of the earth. That's why you find us everywhere across the world. As for the Americas, we were here over 50 thousand years before Columbus. Don't forget about the Moors who traveled from Africa to Europe to assist with the Black Plague, only to be killed and taken advantage of by Satan's gangsters of white supremacy. So we say, "Save us, Lord our God, and gather us from among all the nations, that we may give thanks to your holy name and glory in your praise."

"Then the Lord your God will restore your fortunes and have mercy on you, and he will gather you again from all the peoples where the Lord your God has scattered you. He will raise a signal for the nations and will assemble the banished of Israel and gather the dispersed of Judah from the four corners of the earth. Fear not, for I am with you; I will bring your offspring from the east and the west. In America, I will gather you," declares the Lord, "God who gathers the outcast of Israel. I will gather yet others to him besides those already gathered. I will be found by you," declares the Lord, "and I will restore your fortunes and gather you from all the nations and all the places where I have driven you," declares the Lord, "and I will bring you back to the place from which I sent you into exile."

"Behold, I will bring them from the north country and gather them from the farthest parts of the earth, among them the blind and the lame—spiritually blind, the pregnant woman, and she who is in labor, together—a great company, and they shall return here." Hear the word of the Lord, O nations, and declare it in the coastlands far away. He's only speaking about us, the Black original Israelites, scattered to the four corners of the earth. This evil is something that Satan's gangsters of white supremacy hide because they don't want us to know the truth of our past. They don't want poor Black and poor White to walk into the future that Dr. King dreamed.

(04)

About, let alone letting Blacks know our past alone, because they don't want us to walk into our future of excellence. That's why they steal all our accomplishments, our inventions; they rob us of the knowledge of self so they can create a race of Black Oreo cookies—Black on the outside for perceptionism, with them having a form of Blackness and godliness on the outside but on the inside they KKK. So, there's an agenda to promote genocide on Black on Black mass assassinations through vibrational frequencies, matched through a filter of Satanism. The masses are consumed and hypnotized with false illusions of Christianity, killing one another in the name of "on God." The hip-hop low vibrates Black on one assassination until the mother of a country, melanated body organs, and around the world, Black melaninated body parts and celebrity body ordering harvesting is real also, and all of this is connected with the evilness of Satan's gangsters of the Annunaki and White Supremacy. As we go deeper into ANGELGOONZ, whenever the earth has a problem, you, Black man, Black woman, are the first ones they call on. The only ones they call on because we are the firstborn original people, the oldest on the planet, and they know this. Another thing they won't tell Black people: we are the main conductors; everything down here on Earth, we have all the answers and they know it. That's why they keep us dumb on drugs, etc. Before a booty licker says "nobody makes you do drugs," shut the fuck up; it's all genetically manufactured to be passed down through the mitochondrial DNA, and the US government of Satan's gangsters controlled it all. Please quit running from the truth so you all can continue to benefit off the Black Holocaust. All the immigrants turn a blind eye by design, and in reality, they're complicit 1000%. No offense to Arabs, Mexicans, so-called Native Americans, etc. Go ahead, but when we wake up, don't stop us because no one on the planet has ever been or is still being done as dirty as the Black man, woman, and child. Muslims come into our communities in the name of Allah and sell liquor, beer, pork, whatever, buy Black vagina, go back home, send money back home; they love their people. All other races love their people, but they kill Black people every day by killing his people whom they know the history and all our pain more than we do because they all helped to put us in this condition. So they say Allah and have a form of Allah, but by their exemplifications of Allah, speaks a different tune. I'm not talking about it because we're talking about a Black nation who has been made to fail. Many of us Black people had and still have white supremacy going to work on an evil plan before many of us, all of us, were even born. The plan of genetically modified drugs was being manufactured to create war among each other, and everyone else knows this except you, Black man, and you, white man, that is poor like many of us. They don't want poor Black and White to get along; they only desire a rich society. But how is that possible to wipe us all out? They're trying, but they're losing the battle because God in Heaven is raising up ANGELGOONZ, and no matter what they try, He, God in Heaven, is keeping His word. Just refer to a couple of biblical verses: "He, God in Heaven, inspired me to share with you."

Now, "come on," come on. Common sense! They call on us, the firstborn, the crew, the true, the "Daughters of Isis," and our sons. So, the 12 daughters of Isis are the 12 priests who got the same psychological "connectivity" to their mom as their little brother. But many don't know anything about that because many have been allowed to "misconstrue" the stories by telling us their vision through their vision for us. With a cross, they literally use to cross us all out every day, downplaying the mind of a spiritual people. Their vision, television, and their "manipulation" of the "scriptures" with a scrambled "perspective." While they tell you about 12 disciples, he's telling you "GOD" is telling you, "Them my 12 sisters." And when they tell you about 12 sons of Jacob, these are the ones talking about, "These my 12 brothers."

And all of this is so disturbing. So, when you look at scripture and then you look at hip-hop, originally made to bring us together because music is so vibrational and frequency-driven on energy, that Satan's gangsters in white supremacy are weaponizing it consistently with low vibrational frequencies to kill, steal, and destroy. What are they doing? They are giving all this money, millions that they print out of thin air because "Nixon" took away the "gold standard." Because there isn't any more gold at Fort Knox or anywhere to back the "money" in which they print it out of thin air, giving all this money to a generation whom they made the mothers and fathers drunks with the Arabs' liquor stores on every corner, drugs also from the government, children born addicted like me, and many don't know why. But whatever you put into your body, you put into your children's bodies. And all of this has produced backstabbers, Oreo cookies, and booty lickers of white supremacy, booty licking, buck jumping, and all this money to rappers who are addicted and don't know why. And all this money, they go buy jewelry because that's passed down through the mitochondrial DNA as well. We come from royalty, but they, "the enemy," won't teach rappers a trade in investing or knowledge fully about the growth and development of starting businesses to grow the family. No, Satan's gangsters want you running back to them for all the answers that we already have ourselves. "Entrepreneurship." Ultimately, what they are doing, "Beloved," is countering the balance of GOD in Heaven and Nature, period, with all this poisoning physically and spiritually. And hip-hop and entertainment in Hollywood are something that really don't mix unless it exemplifies what it is to be Christ-like. But how can they exemplify Christ-like when everything they exemplify goes against GOD in Heaven? And many sell their souls in that regard, and buck jumping, waking in strange parties, booty hole sore, and they rapping about being gangsters. Yeah, Satan's gangsters of GOLD, OIL, DRUGS. Their new GOD: GOLD, DRUGS. And white supremacy steals and keeps all the oil, so-called negroes don't get none, no oil. So, rappers get the money and drugs and feel good about that glitter and play, and white supremacy Satan's gangsters get it all with your booty hole and your soul. Oh yeah, booty hole gangsters go to hell. They need them down there with them too, so they can continue the hell for all eternity.

But speaking about Hollywood, what in heaven, I mean hell, are you in Her Woods for? With a "Z." Because if you're not careful, that's the end of you. That's why they killed Young Dolph; he kept his booty hole and his soul. And many others who try to awaken the black, poor, and white community. Before we sell our souls, we would rather die. That's me also. So, get out of her woods because it's been proven long ago that they, in their own words, "hang niggers." Now, it doesn't have to mean literally because they give you enough sex, dope, evil Satan worshipping, forgetting all about Jesus, but you got a cross on your neck, rapping sore, and Satan rituals.

.   .   .

(64)

They are just like their father, Satan, who was a liar in the beginning and a liar now. We just keep following the 70 "TRUTH" because the truth doesn't need any help. The "organic natives" of the land are originally Black, so-called "Negros," who had long since travelled from Africa to the Americas by sea willingly because we are the original navigators of the sea and everything else, except the gun. And the gun is law, and that's why they were successful with the Anunnaki and our ancestors. GOD in Heaven knows the truth, and that's why they don't want you to know the truth because they stole our land. And those Blacks of old told the truth, and even now, we know the truth doesn't need any help.

We are dealing with Satan's gangsters who believe they are going to win this war so much that they are building bigger weapons of firepower to fight GOD in Heaven, with Satan's fallen angels assisting white supremacy and Oreo cookies helping Satan to the fullest. So, Satan's got some gangsters, but GOD's got some goonz from "A" to "Z" – "ANGELGOONZ"

by Minister Melvin A. P.D. T.A.

.   .   .

Many don't know anything about worshipping Satan other than killing one another. So how can you love Christ when they are crossing you out and you are crossing your own people and self "out"? Millions of dollars in jewellery around your neck, and you could start a Black bank with a million dollars and really do something for your people, Black and white. But white people don't do that stupid stuff; they just teach you that so you can be stupid because they know you will fall for anything since you've never had anything. They took it from you and then sold it back to you.

Let's go deeper. One plus two on your right is three, and plus two on your left is three, and if you're going to balance it out, it's three and three: 33. All you need is a third more of an increase, but that's just an "honourable" degree because as soon as you end up at one degree higher, you are frozen asses up, stuck up a creek at 32 degrees Scottish Rite double free "masonry" – the double-headed eagle. And if you don't believe what I am writing, then go prove me wrong. Do your own research, then we can all grow together in peace and overall truth. Cut the damn head off of the two-headed eagle because the eagle only has one head. Inherit the mother's line and the father's line by "Earth's" right and birthright.

And I can't stress enough about the "mitochondrial" right to inherit because it is all passed down through the "mitochondrial" DNA through the "mother" solely and only. Remember "God" and "Christ." Many believe Christ is a woman because we all come from a woman. We are carried in the womb of a woman for nine months. I was born a premature baby because of the drugs implemented into my parents' communities during the civil rights movement to subjugate Blacks and keep us down. And it worked by design way before I was even born. A plan was already working on me from white supremacy, like many of my peers. We all come from a female in life, all of us in all forms, because a female is needed from the originality of the creation of life, which is why many believe Christ is a woman.

A patriarchal right to "rule" is why the main reason the "Y" chromosome, X chromosome, X marks the spot, and Y is the variable to "overstand." Don't understand no hate as taught to control and wipe out the masses through population control. We must "understand" nothing but "God" in Heaven because we are under Him and overstand all righteousness in the godly order of things naturally. But Y is still the question. Well, Satan's got some gangsters. God got some goonz from "A" to "Z" – "ANGELGOONZ"

by Minister Melvin A.P.D.T.A.

.   .   .

"ANGELGOONZ"BY"MINISTER MELVIN".

From kings and queens to things without dreams, it's important for us to always "move" on our own "accord" with our own abilities, with God in heaven, with our own skills, our own gifts for the benefit of self-love because everybody else loves each other except "us" Black people. We must stay on our own level, and I'm told it costs a little over a million to start a bank. Why not pool our resources together and open our own banks? Even if 12 investors chip in, including rappers, we can turn around a lot of this mess overnight. But we must always stay ready to keep from getting ready.

As long as you are successful and buying bling bling, renting mansions, and buying jewellery from everybody else, the immigrants who they now let in so freely due to their lack of reproducing offspring, and don't buy or build anything for your own communities, you are a rich Black slave. They are happy about you because you don't truly own anything. What they do is "nice" your ass for a few long years, sometimes tolerating you, and then, after you've become great and want to do something decent for your people, they "blackball" you, rob you in courts, humiliate you because they own you, disgrace you in front of your own people, and spit you out. They kill you or find another slave to own and exploit. Just don't try to own too much like that, and they consider you an uppity nigger when you stick up for your rights. In the end, you have sold out your own race, and when you need us Blacks that kept it real, the ones you left behind, many leave their Black women they started out with when they were poor and go to uplift their former oppressors, intermarrying into the white race. It's okay, they say, but then when something happens, the first ones they come for or blame is the Black man or woman.

So we must be careful of hateful white supremacists who feel betrayed when they see their race mixing. They go nuts, and many are on the police force, and they take all their frustrations out on Blacks and whites that are involved. They just don't say anything about it. These white supremacist police stations know exactly who they are hiring because they sit across from them every day at the dinner tables. Instead of having a conversation about what's bothering them in white supremacy, there is no communication. Then, next thing you know, their children run up in a school full of hate with a gun, killing people, mainly whites in some cases, and then running up in Black supermarkets, killing Black inventors and Blacks in Texas and all across. We witness this hate. On top of that, we have to deal with the "Oreo" cookie and the booty lickers kissing white ass for instant gratification and then mistaking that "instant gratification" for the holy spirit.

Booty lickers and Oreo cookies will set you up, kill you, and betray you, all in hopes of going to white heaven where they imagine lying around on clouds and trees in mansions, getting fed grapes for the good job they did on earth betraying their own people. Meanwhile, we have some white people on earth that are "blacker" than some "Black" people we know because they exemplify real love from the heart, where your brother, the Oreo cookie, will strike you, cut you down, never wanting to see you grow, selling his or her soul for gold or platinum, and doing nothing for their own.

Instead of coming together as Black people, I find that white people may stick us all in the back under "white supremacy," but ten times out of ten, it will be a "Black" person that sticks "a" Black "in" the "back" first. When we all begin to realize truthfully what these "Satan's gangsters" of white supremacy are doing to create a rich, controllable Oreo cookie society for the rich and population control, everybody acts slow, but this evil is acting and coming fast. As it all begins to play out in reality and changes our lives, we must change our perspective and not lose our focus. Remember, "we change our perspectives to change our lives to save our lives."

We have to truly believe and trust in all the power we truly have, along with all the genuine white people out there who want to live in peace. We would be amazed if we all truly came together to serve God in Heaven. It's okay if we come together to grow together, but the powers that be and those who desire a race war recognize that war is money. They are stupid because war on your own is evil and should be looked upon as evil. They should have all learned something from the Civil War, but we are dealing with a government and a rich world that loves animals more than Black people and poor whites who are in sincere solidarity with us, ANGELGOONZ.

We must recognize the power we have and start using it. It's called common sense and the reality of God, which is in all essence "common sense." Come on, come on, come on, "common sense," come on, come on, it's your often first mind. That's why they say go into the dark; the ancestors say go into the dark because it's in this darkness that we "simulate" being in the very center of our Creator with our Creator. We must remember that first there was darkness, and then God in Heaven said, "Let there be light." And then you must remember your "blackness" and "never be ashamed" of the blackness from which all "life" came. All things come and came from this because we are the original inventors of everything in the beginning. From all this "blackness" and "darkness," white supremacy of Satan's gangsters hates is the same "beautiful" darkness that makes you great.

While that's great, melaninated body parts are big business.

I mean, I know that God says, "I know your trials and tribulations, but you are rich." I didn't think He meant our organs too, but Satan's gangsters and all "wannabe white" people of all races, besides the original chosen by heart from God, from the dark, with a black loving heart, hair of wool, skin of bronze, feet of burnt brass—the heart of the God spoken of in Revelation. The enemy with the white heart is the enemy rider of the "pale white horse" of Satan's gangsters of white supremacy with the cross to cross out all God's people of color, white and black, in Armageddon. So remember, everything starts in the dark. They just want to keep us in a different type of dark; it's called deep sleep.

In tripping darkness while "manifesting" our best life from God, that's what we're talking about—sometimes going into the closet to pray in darkness. Also, blind these demons and evil spirits with the pure light of Almighty God's brightness as the mountains tremble and rumble with God in the midst. Not for them to exploit, but for us to hold on to and to give our babies greatness and provide more than the ability needed to show our babies how to flourish in the face and presence of oppression from an evil oppressor of white supremacy disguised as Christianity.

Because the only real color that matters is the color green until they decide to get on some good old boy nigger stuff. It's real out here, and I don't want our enemies to be able to capitalize off of our downfalls, which they created in the first place—every time creating confusion and division. The next thing you know, everybody is fighting for nothing and nobody knows why, and they are stealing our come-ups every day, our inventions, etc. Because they also have capital gain in taxes—we didn't in the past and really don't now, so we're still overtaxed. They knew about copyrights, but we didn't, and many still don't know about copyright laws or publishing. All this hell in music and especially hip-hop—they handsomely exploit our beloved brothers and sisters in hip-hop, sell their souls and booty holes. The booty and the doodie. And I don't even have to tell you which imposter race runs the music industry; it's the so-called intelligent, wise ones that run everything from the Oreo...

75

Cookie football players and basketball players, all the way to the Oreo cookie music moguls, who sell their souls and then flash millions of dollars in the face of our babies without any training or investment strategy to help plan a good future. They show our rappers how to go to work on a plan for their future after rap, before a plan goes to work on them. They sell their soul all because they want "more" after that initial "advance" runs out.

Allegedly, everything I say is allegedly, and is to be used for entertainment purposes only. It is to entertain you and inspire you enough to do your own research and to arrive at your own individual "truth," so help you God in Heaven. We have to learn all this in order to stay on top of all the Satan's gangsters' bullshit.

Most of the evil associated with robbing us of everything acts as if we just allowed them to steal everything. We didn't; we had no power against them. They had the Anunnaki from the beginning of their inception and fall from grace, losing all melanin and complete rebellion of God in Heaven. Everything God in Heaven says not to do, "they" do at a very high level, even if they have to go under the kitchen sink to make it. This is why rappers feel the need to sacrifice themselves like "Young Dolph" because he knew what true hell was like, and so he worked hard every day to show us all how to work independently and own our own.

Satan's gangsters of white supremacy, booty lickers, Oreo cookies, the Black KKK, took him out, assassinated him. Initially, Young Dolph turned down 22 million dollars and got shot 22 times. It was all a catch 22. He offered someone 2 million for a verse, divide that 2 into 222—

numbers don't lie, 666. There's some evil stuff going on down there in Memphis, and it reeks of the Black KKK police department also involved in the Tyre Nichols case of an unarmed black man lynched by KKK activity. The only thing the white K is known for exemplifying is now being exemplified by Black KKK officers, who have since been fired.

As soon as we take complete control of our communities and keep fighting to get rid of all this buffoonery, we can really go to work on a plan. Understanding that it is all in the secret of mass assembly—the love, the loyalty, no outside interference from Satan's gangsters of white supremacy sowing dissension. The holdup is that there aren't enough of us to stand up. The ones with money and riches want to go and buy millions in jewelry from jewelers that don't even look like them. Nothing wrong with that, but they killed Duke the Jeweler, a prominent young black jeweler from Chicago. They just assassinated him in Houston. And Takeoff of the Migos—it was supposed to be some real street gangsters in Houston who were supposed to have their backs but didn't. They were both robbed of their life, and God in Heaven knows only what else.

But when the real gangsters of white supremacy showed up, all these so-called G's put their hands behind their backs. On top of all this BS to deal with, we come to wake up and find God's revelation coming true. He is restoring us, but we have been swapped out and replaced. They got other people over here pretending to be us, brought over here and let come over here, and call them Indians. In fact, we are the Indians before the Indians. We were already here, many hundreds of thousands of us, for over 50,000 years. We just didn't have any "guns" when they came, nor the artillery or means to properly defend ourselves. Black men, black women, and black children were taken over and put to sleep forcibly, like a little baby put to sleep on a knee—a knee of white supremacy. They work hard every day to keep us that way, making it hard for most blacks to own something.

But the booty licker and Oreo cookies of white supremacy will always kill, steal, and destroy any dream or growth for us all who are "authentic" in God's love in Heaven. For His true, regardless of color, God knows the true color of the heart. It is wise not to follow Satan and his followers who offer you money for your soul. Remember...

ANGELGOONZ FROM "A"TO"Z" BY MINIS-TER"MELVIN"A"P"D"T"A"

while many of our own kind Who Betray Us for money coonishish who look just like us "Meaning"

Reprobated "MIND" OREO-COOKIES, morally depraved, unprincipled, "BAD" "SO-CALLED" "Mohos" and "NEGROS," backstabbers, backdoorers of the worst kind, rejected by "GOD" in "HEAVEN." SOUL SELLERS beyond hope of salvation, they are and are of a "CROSS" that crosses you out if you trust them. As soon as the bullshit they help create hits the fan, they are the first ones to say, "I'm a Christian, I go to church, I ain't did nothing wrong." Meanwhile, somebody has been killed behind their scheming like the devil. In fact, they are the devils. They have their own devil god, Satan, but they are part of Satan's body—think the arms of Satan—because there are many of them hoping to be accepted as white or alike. Damn, get over it—you're black. Nahhh, I mean, you're right—you're white in your mind.

The Bible teaches us that those kinds of people are what is referred to as fair-seeming glitter and play followers, dilly-dilly, dolly-wishey washy, harshy-type, self-hated and reprobated. The Bible puts it like this, as "GOD" speaks, "For as he thinketh in his heart, so is he." Proverbs 23:7: "Eat and drink, saith he to thee; but his heart is not with thee." So yes, they are a cross between Uncle Toms and Mammies, "PussyFootz" from "P" to "Z." "PUSSYFOOTZ" literally.

As far as the good Black woman and good intentional Toms, there were some who sacrificed, and Black women have always been the true sacrificers, always giving so much to white supremacy and to her Black family every day. In the past, during all our struggles as a people, for that we owe her a whole lot of respect. Far too often, the Black woman is forgotten about her sacrifices, so many that she is the only woman on earth since the creation of time who has given up so much—everything except her soul, because she belongs to "GOD" and is GOD of all the Black nation "ONLY." White supremacy knows this, and that's why they give us so much hell, because race and civil wars are pure hell, and all who participate are a "hellish people" "VOID" of GOD, unless GOD in Heaven says so.

From kings and queens to things that nobody wants to have anything to do with but Satan, and he's making slaves out of them every day. Aside from that, we must not forget the fact that history hides her true story because white supremacy tells his vision through television as well. Evil cover-ups by "Satan's Gangsters" of long-term schemers with solidarity to stay supreme in evil, masters of illusions and delusions. We had the "Gullah" wars when we, and the ancestors, teach us and taught us. Yes, I said taught and then I said "teach us" because they continue to teach us. The fact is that they are in us, and our genes are so connected, and we are in tune with them that know-how. But when white supremacy tells her story, she doesn't call it the Gullah wars; she is a thief, America. She, the mother whore, calls it "The Seminole Wars," so you can know the difference by hearing it when you're hearing it. The sisters in the know the truth we need to see.

What modernization should look like in terms of all the land that was stolen from us—I mean, these are some dirty-ass gangsters of the "Booty" and the "Doodie." Many of us don't even know how to properly access or assert the fact that we, as natives, are the original natives of this land. Yes, because we were here over 50,000 years before anyone else learned and stole everything from us. That's why they engaged in that massive transatlantic slave trade, mainly to the Americas. Yes, some of us, many of us, did come that way, but the vast majority of us were already here. We were just too trusting of people and fell out of God's grace. God felt crossed by idol worshipping, so we were allowed to be crossed out by the cross people and master crossers, with orders from the Pope decreeing, "Make them accept the cross or die."

But the fact is, God knows what we do not, and He has come back for us. We are waking up by the hundreds of thousands, and the fact of the matter is that we can and will reclaim our land. They know this; that's why they're selling it and giving it all away. But it doesn't matter what they do with the land because God is the man, the real man, so to speak. Literally, this is hallowed land that they bastardized and whorish, damn whores, man whores, and man whores in this white supremacy world of greed. When you don't need it, it's greedy evil shit they relish in. All who desire to be in bed with the "Mother Whore" are her tricks, and they all sell and sold their soul for gold, silver, platinum, for glitter and play, straight tricks pimped by the mother whore, tricked by tricknology.

But now, come on, they can't just hold onto our land forever because common sense should tell them nothing lasts forever. They hijacked our land and our plan. You can't count on the media because they've been bought and paid for by impostors on our land, the so-called Indians and the damn pilgrims talking about the year 1620, called Plymouth. Damn liars, we were already here in the Americas 50 to 100,000 years prior to Columbus. That's why you can't find any slave ships, only a few, so to speak.

And aside from all of that, as well, we have to keep videotaping white supremacist cops and Oreo cookie cops who turn the other cheek. We have to hold them responsible on video and let the whole world see and the courts judge. But it's still not enough as good Black and white people come together to try. We must try harder and keep our heads on a swivel at all times. It's simply just not enough to do when there is more work to be done to enhance a brighter world for our offspring coming up behind us. We can't allow this evil of hate in white supremacy to tear down our interracial families because it's here, and we're here to stay.

Now, Mr. Charlie, get your white racist ass out of the way and go find another damn game to play on yourself. Because according to the scriptures, you lose. And this is true.

I say it's not enough to control the land; however, our control is in informing the rich among us if they will listen and agree not to continue to sell their souls because they're still here for a reason. We must talk to all the chiefs over the land, all the lands, and agree to take on no family beef because pork's the enemy. They're the ones who taught you and me, through our parents, who were lied to and blessed it, as evil as it is, a meat and to bless white supremacy. Satan's gangsters taught us to bless it all in the name of the cross, eat this death in the name of Christ, like as if Christ would condone this. That's just like taking a big pot of alkaline water because it's healthy and then putting cyanide, pork, and salt in it and then saying, "Eat."

We must rebuild our family structures around and current family life.

· · ·

With whoever we're with, we have a history on all sides, and the truth needs to be free and told. But often, at a price, we're going to lose some friends; we're going to lose some family because of us wanting to do the right thing. But we must remember, we do the right thing not because it's something to do, but because it's the God in Heaven thing to do. Build a matriarchal world society of peace where the woman is the head right beside the man, never second.

Learn the tablets of the individual in the family; the top job at that point is to know who to put on the family board, to trust with the competence of God in Heaven, denouncing all evil. And using the same formula that corporate America white supremacy used to take us over, only this time, God in Heaven has heard and accepted our plea and repentance. He is with us all, especially His Angelgoonz because we are doing and have been doing the work, including those of us that He has awakened as His Angelgoonz, and apply happiness to the family, love to the family from the heart because what comes from the heart touches the heart and the family to bank on is the family that won't steal from us, that won't deny us our own bank.

Whites already have their own banks that lie and cheat and steal every day. What's wrong with our own banks on a high level? Black banks and interracial world-known banks, let's be the first to name it that openly. God has told me, and then the whole world will see the realness of the truth. And our own banks won't hurt us for the enemy once they see we're all on code. So when the national debt turns around, they turn off the accounts, close all the accounts, and they—white supremacy—pay up, pay us. It's galactic law, science, and mathematics and numbers don't lie. But mainly, the prostitutes and the church need to come together, same think tank and apply it to ourselves. After all, the purpose is to take out the central banks whom America borrowed all that money from to start and fight all these wars to fight over who would steal, kill, and destroy as many of us as they could.

And they borrowed it all from the Jewish people, Rome, etc. Everybody played a major role in our downfall as a black nation. We're not imbeciles; we have good teachers over here at the house under God in Heaven. We know and are continuing to learn the truth. And nothing but the truth else we don't want it. And when the real church and mosque settle y'all's accounts, they must settle the old ones too, because plain and simple, Satan's got some gangsters. God's got some goonz from A to Z, Angelgoonz

by Minister Melvin A.P.D.T.A., Angelgoonz.

. . .

ANGELGOONZ FROM"A"TO"Z".......BY MINISTER "MELVIN"A. P.D.T.A."..

As we build and strive for power, every avenue that leads to power has an imposter ready to knock you over or keep you in line. "Watch what you darkies say," "watch what you darkies do," at all times. Truth be told, there is no successful Black person without a Jewish leader. Plain and simple, they are a successful, smart, crafty, intelligent people, reaching great heights despite all they have been through. But for the life of me, I can't get over all the money they have. All these Jewish people—old Jewish women, someone's moms and dads—are on commercials talking about saving the Jews, hungry, homeless, on TV asking, begging for money. When they are the most successful people on the planet, why won't they help their own people? Begging for our money, it's crazy.

But I know why. The only color that matters to them is Jews with money and darkies who can make money on the plantation field of sports. "Stay good, darkies," "be a good boy," "be a good girl," you little Black "witch." Replace the "W" with a "B," that's how they talk and view us. Sad, beloved, that's how many of them feel in white supremacy. "Run fast, nigger," "dribble fast, nigger," hop around like a bunny rabbit as a fapper and wear pink and white flower sweaters. I don't know, but I'm told that their buttholes are sore from too much rapping and dabbing, and extra rapper-dapper curriculum activities, so they're backstabbing for real. Literally setting each other up, backdooring each other. All they've got to do is turn it around and come to God in Heaven and stop following the god of this world, Satan, and his minions. Because when you say something they don't like, they cut you off.

The Constitution of the United States has been under attack for a very long time, and all the people in power bow to a higher power. Any president selected is not the boss; he has to go behind the backdoor to get permission from the shadow government. It seems the synagogue of Satan has ruined the country, and we pray they have not ruined the world. As I think back through history, I see how great leaders like Billy Graham and President Carter tried to stop them, to no avail. Billy Graham and Nixon said they didn't have the power to stop them, probably because of all the money America had to borrow to fight wars. The powers that be aim to stop America in her tracks because America saw what was happening to the Jews and their Holocaust, just as they —America—participated in our Black Holocaust. Interestingly enough, they all fail to talk about the Blacks in Germany during this time, the Nazi persecution of Black people.

When the Nazis came to power in 1933, several thousand Black people were living in Germany. They were harassed, persecuted because the Nazis didn't believe in or cherish Black people; they viewed Black people as inferior, racially inferior. While there was no centralized systematic program targeting Black people for murder, many were imprisoned, forcibly sterilized, and murdered by the Nazis simply for being Black. Understanding pure hate and not understanding Satan's gangsters and white supremacy because they were treated that way for being Black. The international bankers and the Rothschilds, most famous in all of Europe and the world, run Europe's economy and political destiny, staying behind the scenes.

Years ago, you couldn't find Jews anywhere out front because darkness loves darkness. But there are two types of darkness: the darkness of the soul where God in Heaven always is, and the darkness of evil, the darkness of fair-seeming glitter and play, the negative energy that leads to falsehood and complete downfall. They were always in the background because they didn't want anybody to know they were running everything. But the damn fools should have known all of this because it's in all the scriptures that God didn't allow them to tamper with. If you catch them doing something wrong and bring it up, since they control everything, they come after you in the name of evil, camouflaged with the cross, and call you anti-Semitic. But they're anti-Semitic in the first place. All this wickedness going

Against God in Heaven to please their 'god' on 'earth' for their hope, the Pope. For a country that claims Jesus, you can't get mad because there are two Jesus Christs: the true Christ and the one that white supremacy created. Why don't they exemplify what it is to be Christ from God in Heaven? Instead of the evil that's being exemplified by the white powerful elite, all you have to do is look on YouTube and do your own research to dig for the truth. Sometimes the truth comes at the ultimate price of life. I ain't scared, and neither were many of my ancestors. Damn it.

So, America's doom is approaching, and there are many who really don't know why, and many who don't care, and many who don't want to know the truth, especially the guilty. It is the express purpose of the coming of God in Heaven because their 6000-year rule is up, to make manifest the sins of the people whom he will destroy. Because America represents herself as a God-fearing country, but which 'God'? Which means they are followers of Christ and has become crystallized in one: the Father, the Son, and the Holy Ghost. They profess to be a country of peace-loving people, but today America's doom is set. John the Revelator said it like this: 'Babylon,

Babylon, Revelation 18:2, and she has become a habitation of devils and a home of every foul spirit and a cage for every unclean bird.' A devil is one who knows God in Heaven and does the very opposite of what God in Heaven or Sodom and Camor Ingeneats 19:128 follows Satan's gangsters. It's wrong, and you've been tricked. It's called tricknology, and they have been tricking all who follow and don't wake up.

We're either going to be right or we are going to be wrong. We're going to be what God the Father said or we're going to be Satan, 'Dead'. The war of Armageddon is to decide who lives and who dies on this earth, and spiritually my mission is to expose Satan's gangsters in white supremacy camouflaged and covered under the cross. My mission is to uncover Satan so that we all can fall away from Satan and fall into the loving, compassionate arms and hands of God in Heaven, so that we can all escape the doom of this world of white supremacy. Satan's gangsters. Our role is not to fight, and we don't have anything worth fighting with anyway, so don't fool yourselves with glitter and play because the real men and women of God in Heaven are here to stay.

But if we got the truth, and we do have the truth, that's what frightens them. Satan's afraid of that because then that means he has to go to hell with only a few. Then he plotted don't follow him don't believe in him don't follow people that teach you little bitty sins because little bitty sins graduate to big sins, and the devil is a liar and a deceiver. We must be the precious cornerstone of God in Heaven, holding up the glory of God, praising God in Heaven. Only the Jews say never again, and damn right I'm with them, never again for what they went through, knowing that life of the oven. Why create a spiritual oven for blacks to watch blacks burn in? Well, okay, but they can say that all they want to, but the scriptures say it like this in the Bible: 'Behold the day burns like an oven and leaves them neither root nor branch, Malachi 4:1.' For the 411 information numbers don't lie. All will turn into powder.

The war of Armageddon is to see who will live on this earth because you can't live on the earth, which was made for righteousness and continue to do all this damn evil and turn a blind eye continually and think God in Heaven won't punish you. But when God whoops you, you will know it's God whooping you, not because he hates you, but because he loves you. Now trust me, you would rather the whooping from God instead of a whooping from Satan because often Satan's whoopings lead to dying, death in sin, physically and spiritually straight to hell. God in Heaven loves us and doesn't want us to go down with Satan and his gangsters, the powerful white supremacy, because God is not unjust. When he kills you, you know you deserve it.

Four presidents threatened the international banking systems by their focus on what the Constitution defines as money owed by their efforts to limit their debt the country owed to private bankers 'Each' may have paid the ultimate price for doing so and so doing starting with President Lincoln with America facing a financial crisis due to the spiral cost of the Civil War Lincoln and Congress passed the 1st Legal Tender Note 'ACT'. Authorizing the Secretary of"

Treasure 150 million dollars in United States notes. Now that's a challenge to the international bankers who loaned America the money to fight all these racist wars. The sad part is these were notes that were not backed by gold or silver. Because they were issued into circulation directly through the United States Treasury, they did save the nation from having to pay high interest on an oppressive debt controlled by the international bankers. On April 14, 1865, President Lincoln was assassinated.

President James Garfield, focusing on and preserving the monetary system envisioned by the Constitution five years before he became president, wrote in February: "Coins of finite ascertained weight duly stamped and authenticated by the government is the only safe standard of money currency, and no form of credit is safe unless it is convertible into coins at the will of the holder." When he became president in 1881, he continued to advocate for the gold standard. He only served as president for six months, and on September 19th, President Garfield was assassinated.

President William McKinley, also a longtime supporter of the gold standard, signed the Gold Standard Act into law on March 14th, 1900, 123 years ago. That law set the price of the dollar to gold for the next 34 years until President Roosevelt devalued the dollar and withdrew gold from public circulation. On September 14th, 1901, he was assassinated.

President John F. Kennedy, on June 4th, 1963, signed Executive Order #11110, which instructed the Secretary of the Treasury to issue silver certificates against any silver bullion, silver, or standard silver in the Treasury, introducing silver-backed currency. President Kennedy was creating a direct rivalry to the paper currency of the Federal Reserve. On November 22nd, President John F. Kennedy was assassinated.

As we see how evil Satan's gangsters are, we have to understand how evil they truly are to us and to themselves in the end. But more importantly, as we move on into what it is we need to be doing for ourselves and leave Satan to his own demise, as a people of all races, especially the downtrodden black communities, we need to understand that family structure is family wealth building. No doubt understanding how to distribute funds adequately, there will be counselors available teaching modules on family banking and family training all the time.

As a people, we need to teach how to handle wealth right. So, it will be available through the Small Business Administration; that's what they will be repurposed for, not for wicked cheese, nip, Oreo-cookie activities. Not for business, but for family banking. All of this is so damn essential for us to grow and not become an anchor of finding no excuses. We are only entitled to what we earn, and that's what we must make fit our lives, our lifestyle, our budget, because that's what you like, good pride, and that's what we work for, and that's what we're all willing to die for.

With high ambition and putting in all the necessary work, without white supremacy, slavers, and slave masters are bitches. So, we let them continue being evil bitches because when it comes back around to them, they will still be evil bitches. Easy bitches who feel they need slaves of all kinds to get richer and survive as rich people often do, the evil rich population control selfish bastards who only want a world of the white rich and Oreo-cookie rich to live in.

But ain't they missing something? Because there will always be poor people, because the rich will not always stay rich, and constantly getting ahead by body organ harvesting and modern-day slavery as well is big business. All this is evil, and that's what our open enemies understand. But God in Heaven desires us to understand these demons and to always be on the lookout for the helpers in the church, on the streets, the good ones, not the ones that mistake ass-kissing and instant gratification for the holy.

Spirit" because the church, the mosque, the temple all have their plants, booty lickers, backstabbers, Oreo-cookies, and snitches. Speaking of "snitching," Adam was the first snitch; he snitched on his wife to God, and they both fell into sin. They weren't supposed to be intermingling with the trees of other people who follow Satan's gangsters. They were supposed to stay with their own trees and messed around and found the wrong tree of PCP. Satan's got some gangsters, God's got some "goonz" from "A" to "Z" Angelgoonz

by Minister Melvin A.P.D. T.A.

We continue to go deeper and deeper, but Father God up in Heaven gave me the best advice this morning. He said, "Nahhh, we haven't gone far enough, beloved." I asked, "What do you mean, Lord God?" He said, "Enki and the Sumerian tablets tie to white supremacy and Satan's gangsters." I said, "Whoaaaaaaa," and I began to study as He (God) talked, even about the Black Knight Satellite. I listened and wrote.

The Black Knight Satellite, and please remember, we are taught black is evil, but it's not. The Black Satellite is still orbiting the Earth, and we understand that it is intelligently made. Thus, the Messengers of AngelGoonZ communicate through different frequencies. This Black Knight is somehow correlated with the constellations, and many wonder how or why the government won't bother or mess with it because they mess with everything else. Why not mess with the Black Knight Satellite, you damn Satan's gangsters? Because they know better. They don't have a clue truly of what they are dealing with. They are already afraid of the black man awakening, so they damn well don't want to awaken that damn Black Knight. It's black, they're scared, and who do they oppress the most? Everything is mathematics with this Black Knight Satellite, and also, everything in Islam is mathematics, but they don't want to talk about that neither because they want and desire you to stay asleep.

They estimate it weighs about 15 tons, and this is just from an estimate from STS-88. When you have something that huge that has the potential to do more harm than you know about, and it's been up there longer than we've had any space program, well, how did it get up there? All we do know is it is providing an accurate GPS location, literally providing a GPS location in the Epsilon Biotus constellation, and it is all owned by Enlil of the Sumerian Tablets. We have a record of beings known as the Annunaki on Earth having a deep connection to or even ownership of the Biotus constellation.

Then we have this device up there, the Black Knight Satellite, and then the NSA discovers this signal and decodes it, giving up the location of what the Biotus constellation is doing. So, in all essence, we have three constellations here, and since they don't know who these people are and what they are doing, it would be wise to leave them alone because you don't want no smoke with their God in Heaven and rush Armageddon. Suppose it has a defense mechanism? Why wouldn't it? So they don't want to go pushing or probing it at all. Damn Satan's gangsters of white supremacy may bring on a bigger power than they are prepared to deal with. Why rush scripture? Trust me, these devils and demons do not wish to be disturbed or rushed to the Day of Judgment awakened before time. So they just call it leftover space trash floating around with GPS technology better than theirs. There...

. . .

Are UFOs up there that are real? That's something we must understand. There's a threat of propaganda to promote fear in the masses to control people through fear, pumping into you once you're programmed by their vision through television. They can control you better, raising your cortisol and all your hormones, and dopamine, and everything else. Now here comes the way for them to drug you, dope you up, continuing to put messiahs to sleep sent to awaken the sleeping giants, the Black race. The agenda is money; they have an evil system of white supremacy going around the whole world and 8 billion people to confuse by Satan's gangsters.

However, information encoded onto the waves of television, through your eyes, your ears, is set through the retina to the back of the brain, sorts it all out, then reads the programming codes. The programming codes trigger your response and put you in fear, making you afraid of Satan's gangsters. This fear is how your brain gets sucked to the back, all that blood, and now you're not able to make good decisions. That's when they turn you into an addict, a zombie, and most victims of Agent Orange can tell you more about that sincerely.

As America believes in killing people to pay her bills, which she created with all this damn war, to pay your bills in honor of God in Heaven. But they don't pay their bills in honor of God in Heaven; they pay their bills with evil, with the innocent blood of Black people always on the front lines in all their wars, only to come home to be called n-word and lynched in modern times, even to this very day. So, they pay their bills in honor of Satan, their god on Earth, endowed in white supremacy, and they're doing all this hell on Earth. And they wonder why it's up there? The Black Knight Satellite watching and recording everything.

All of this robbing other nations of their natural resources, fake wars, fake news. I wish all the presidents would have to go to war themselves first, with their families on the front lines, before any citizens should have to. And also, all the police chiefs lose all their pensions if their officers murder unarmed Blacks over racism and KKK activities. I bet you all this evil mess with white supremacy would stop overnight. It will all stop when we all stop playing and participating in their games of tricknology in their matrix. Everything comes to an end, so will their rule of white supremacy, Satan's gangsters. He has some gangsters; God's got some goonz, Angel Goonz.

Enki is known as Nudimmud, Nimsku, God of wisdom, as mentioned before. But the reason I bring this up is because Cain, where did they say he got his wife? South Africa? Enlil, God of command, the term "life-giving water" is something we will get into shortly. The tree, no doubt, represents the male and female principles, stands in the background, and it goes like this: Lord of the Earth, source of the Nile River. Remember when the Bible said they were all on the mounds or levy? Because this is what he was up against. Enki's priest was the one sending the assistance.

Life-giving water is Semitic, and the two streams of water they keep hiding and switching things around to confuse us. It was the Egyptian priest fighting against the Babylonians, all documented in the hieroglyphics. Great doctors and scientists talk about this all the time, just like they all have a Quran in their homes, but they don't want you to have one. However, in the priest wars is what I'm referring to. Sierra Leone, a mean name Albert Church, is said, is an ancient Egyptologist in the 1800s. At least two talked about the secret priest wars behind all the evil unraveling now.

Remember, as we learn, the priest wars were predicated upon something often talked about as we are losing memory left in the iconography of land, in the statuary, in an ark. So now, somebody coming to you telling you that they got your family hostage, right? Follow me now, beloved. You've got to tell your families how to free themselves, but you can't tell them openly. But you get control of all of this right here. What messages are you going to send to let your family know exactly how to get free? Well, listen, you use craft, magic, exorcisms, healing. Now remember, family, when they said that God was a trickster? That means that you couldn't trick them; they can't be deceived. So they have to be damn good in tricknology, mischief makers can't deceive them. Remember, the God of...

(83)

Wisdom, we understand that fresh water is about love, romance here, and then we gain intelligence, intellect, linear logic, father logic, father-line thinking. Now we enter tricknology of the card games, etc., crafts, which include ceramics and designs. Then we move into magic, where we see incantations, spells, and exorcisms, casting out the devil to truly reveal him. Remember, the trickster doesn't want to be seen.

So, the priesthood of Enlil are our moon and unknown priest. Now, look ahead at the beings, look at the Maldekians. These beings were other beings called the Primitives, beloved. They are disagreeable to live with, and they are the ones doing all the kidnapping, the little short beings, the kids are rapping them in mixed with trolls. In Hindu, created these beings, horns and being from Vulcan, like you think Star Trek, they tell us everything in code. Well, Satan's got some gangsters, God's got some goonz, Angel Goonz from A to Z. Angel Goonz

by Minister Melvin A.P.D.T.A. Angel Goonz,

When we talk about elf-shaped ears, many believe that people out here think God in Heaven waking up is something we just made up, like we just made it all up out of the blue. Not recognizing that blue is recessive, even through 20/20 vision. The darker the eyes, the darker the genes, the blacker the skin, the deeper the root, the authenticity of a thing. Everything in life is important because it entails the real identity and origin—originality of a life form—from which all life extends. This is important and should not be a secret, no more than UFOs. Everything on television is a form of "thievery" that they stole from us all. More importantly, this is no watered-down version of speaking the truth. Real men, men of God, are never afraid to die or speak truth to power, and God is raising us up every hour. They stole the knowledge of ours as a people, a great people, and recast it as if it were their knowledge and greatness, assuming another's property and land, men, women, and children who were already here before Columbus, 50,000 to 100,000 years. No, it's our knowledge from our creator, God in Heaven. And only a devil thinks and believes he can hide the knowledge of God from His original people.

Okay, we know according to the Bible, which has been tampered with so much, that we Africans came here, a small portion taken as slaves, but many of us were already here. So now, when they are speaking of Vulcan "VULKIN" like from Star Trek, you know what they are talking about, right? Not the places, the planets, etc. Not L. Ron Hubbard, who wrote a series from our stolen wisdom, knowledge, and understanding as "ANGELGO-ONZ," and he said that a group of them came down and was actually the "ANNUNAKI Chronicles," far from any scientific book, and were thrusted into the "Volcano," and these are the exact same beings called the Vulcanites.

That's how they got their name tied to the unraveling of the truth. Where's the devil today? Black devils are the same devils, the same species that came from the sea. The Bible says, the holy tablets, the beings that came from another planet called Titan, which is the moon to Saturn. They were on Pluto too, while the original species was on Titan. It was knocked out of orbit by "NUBIRU." Nubiru then migrated to Earth, deep down into the Bermuda Triangle. They crashed down and they were, and are, the "disagreeables" to live with in peace, called the primitive ones, and believe me, beloved, they are the direct individuals that were on Pluto too. The holy tablets, and they were the ones the "ANNUNAKI" were trying to convert to being good beings. Not good humans, they were not human, but beings. They were trying to breed them with the original inhabitants of the Earth, as I stated, breed, intermix, but they still came out disagreeable to live with, and that's exactly why we have "The Widow's Peak" pictures, like Edward Wolfgang Munster, to give you a visual description. These are the beings underground. Go google "Wolfgang Amadeus," who was one of the greatest composers, and the picture that they changed to tell their vision, his history says, however, he was half "Moor," original Moor.

So now, I really need you, the reader, to remember who was over "Arts" and "Craft," and then remember "Music" falls under that. Perhaps telling their vision through television, that's why it is believed to be in the TV series, "The Munsters." My question is, why is everything that started out black ending up white? And every time you try to have this conversation about the truth, they call it racist or they say we can't publish this because even though it's the truth, it's racist. Bullshit. The fact is the truth hurts, and America has been nothing in terms of her treatment of blacks but United Snakes of America, who keeps shedding her skin, refusing to change for the better, remaining the same under evil snake skin over and over. But the Bible and Quran, all the scriptures, say,

"Hell will ask, is there any more room?" And God will say yes and give the hypocrites new fresh booty-licking Oreo cookie new skins to replace the burnt-up ones previously burned.

Okay, let's get deep into it. The bow-legged trait comes from them too. Really, it comes from "TOTEM" energy, but I don't want to go too deep into it. For that, you'll have to wait for Hel Mart, my next novel, because I don't want to go too deep and lose you after having just found you. Now you'll see the red, white over blue background. Now Enlil had the double right to rule.

"Right?" Okay, these are the double-headed wings in the middle of the flag, 33 degrees doubled. We learn all this as we track and trace down the family crest. There we find the code flipped and the sign upon actual study: an eagle with a double head facing away from each other.

"MOTHER" LINE and "FATHER" LINE, 32 degrees in the middle. What's very imperative to note is that 3x2=6, but that's another topic. The "Scottish Rite" actually means you have the blood and the right. The handling of the sword is the sworn oath, "Blood" over "War." That's also why in Switzerland, it used to be on one of their flags. You can look all of this up as we understand that

Satan has some gangsters, but "GOD GOT SOME GOONZ."

ANGELGOONZ FROM A to Z by Minister Melvin A.P.D. T.A. ANGELGOONZ FROM A to Z,

ANGELGOONZ

80

As we go on, Enlil's children were trying to use this authority on Earth and the "Galactic Council" said that's not possible, the double-headed bird. But, over here in America, the double-headed "EAGLE" on a flagpole is significant. Don't forget they also have two "Faces" like that of the "OREO-COOKIE" and Booty Lickers of White supremacy—black one minute, then BKKK the next (Black KKK).

It's sad that black people are scared to be themselves, so they brainwashed themselves into believing that "Black" is "Evil" and that they themselves are "White" because they hate "NIGGERS," which by the way is crazy because anybody can be a Nigger acting "Niggardly" in any race. A low life would have to be a low life in order to rob a whole nation of people of the knowledge of self, rape, rob, and kill every avenue for them to remember who they really are just so you can enslave them for your evil gains under Jesus Christ by orders of the Pope and the Queen of England. The British and the Portuguese forced upon a people the worst treatment of all time under the sun, then lied and acted as though it didn't exist and acted as though we blacks were not already here 50,000 to 100,000 years before Columbus.

You will have to be a NIGGER NATION OF PEOPLE to use all this evil on a single race of people and subject them to the worst treatment under the sun ever, then use Jesus Christ to enforce it, then force that religion on those people you robbed of so much, many even their souls. So don't fix your mouth about who and what a "Nigger" is. Black people just need to wake up because the more I dig, the more they shut down certain functions, computers, and all to block knowledge. They don't want y'all to know the truth because the truth will set you free, and the truth doesn't need help. And when it does, that's why they hide it.

Pulling the cover of the truth and running into "Black" screens is an old C.I.A. tactic. Black screens go on the slab whenever we talk about the 32 degrees, they get upset, and that's why it is extremely imperative that we get to the message. That's the cover we pull off their asses. Black secret green, gold, grey, neutral zone B32 3+2 is a pointed star. We are indeed waking up, but to what? And yes, we are "Overstanding" their understanding because God says we are above what they associate us with, and certainly, God is above what they associate with "Him." Meaning He is above all they associate with him, above because she is above all on the Earth, "MOTHER EARTH." And the mother of Earth is the black woman. Like it or not, go do your research. Scientists are coming out and admitting this, and this in no way diminishes the role of all women because all women are the gateway to GOD.

All life came through her. The first woman on Earth. All life started in Africa, full of melaninated people. No recessiveness or weaker genes were seen as leprosy, forbidden, and so the Forbidden have come home to roost. They have been roosting, oppressing all other races on Earth, robbing natural resources. The fantasy world created by Hollywood doesn't make it any better, and the metaverse is full of bullshit somewhat. So should the matriarch be set up according to craft?

First off, let us humbly "Overstand" that the Matriarchs are well-established among Women. The men don't pick the matriarch; the Matriarchs pick each other. The one who gets the most "Matriarchal" "Support" from the other "Matriarchs" becomes the "Lead Matriarch" and her "supporters." So this is something from the woman, passed down, and this is what we call "pyramid" "Mudge" government that overrides the jurisdiction because the first rights boil down to "who owns the rights to the Earth" and our land, not theirs. And whether they like it or not, it's all about the woman.

This is why the 5 Percenters call the Woman "EARTH," and when you hear me talking from time to time about "Mitochondrial," it's in the "Soil." Only the "Woman" has this "Information" to pass down through the "Mitochondrial DNA," and women control all of this "Mitochondrial" by reaching the love "Frequency" and the Anger frequency of AngelGoonZ, the "Frequency" which raises the "Male's" Mitochondrial in their presence. So, in essence, the more good women that a male is around, the "Better" the "Male" will be as men. That is how he becomes his "Divine."

Masculine self by being approved by men and women, most loved and most respected, is the one thing people are pushing to beat the evil in this "Battle" of "From A to Z ANGELGOONZ." The magic touch is acupuncture. How are women supposed to deal with the people that look like women and are not? Well, the answer is women don't have to weed them out; they only need to worry about the real women. That's it. We will know them too because they won't get along with real women. And if there are no real men around, what then?

That's when we turn to the REAL GOOD MEN. Sometimes good men have to go to prison for speaking truth to power and for protecting women, children, and their manhood. The evil men are dealt with by God, even the Oreo Cookie who loves "White Supremacy" and hates his own self and his own people.

Remember, the woman is God's workshop in the womb of "ANGELGOONZ." Since Satan has some gangsters in power, endowed in "White Supremacy," God has some goonz—ANGELGOONZ—to help all of His oppressed.

ANGELGOONZ by Minister Melvin A.P.D.T.A..... ANGELGOONZ

AngelGoonz

Ultimately, these are the ones we have been fighting against the whole time: "Oreo Cookies of Thee Ancients." Remember, the monkey rides on the elephant to spot the snakes, even in these United Snakes of America. It's believed the pope gave America to Spain. Entrustians play a major role in arts and crafts, pottery, and all Entrustian civilization. Red and green simply mean blood and earth. What is imperative to note is that red and green make brown, which is really a reptilian type in the brain—the primate brain, the neocortex. Pay attention to the matrix in real life. Thinking above the waist—higher self, conscience, and constantly becoming awakened daily to the knowledge of self—is to know and learn as much as we can. For the Bible says, "Seek ye knowledge." The lower self is the mammalian brain, the reptilian brain, and "neo" means new. Once overstood through overstanding, you too can master the frequency of the animal totem.

Animal totems are a significant aspect of Native American culture (blacks in America before Columbus) and the $5 Indians. A totem animal is a spiritual symbol of an individual or family according to American Indian beliefs. It's the main guiding spirit that stays with you for life, which is why it's hard to spiritually forget the truth of what happened to us completely before we continue to believe and teach all the lies of evilness to our children. It's all embedded in our DNA. They tried to erase it in this world, but it is not of this world. Your family, throughout a lifetime and its lineage, uses totems to tie in and tell a clearer story of the clans. Holy guardian angels are something else to look up to develop a deeper overstanding or, if you prefer, understanding.

Angel Thelema, the great work, is generally defined as those spirituals leading to the accomplishments of true will of oneself. Every one of us has a guardian angel that comes from us, that we each individually hold. For the Bible says, "Ye are all gods of the most high." This system predates religion, utilizing totem spirits. It's deeper than most and better for someone ascribing to any set religion. Religion is toxic and bad for the soul, but spirituality is better for the soul because it unites the rightly guided—the right.

AngelGoonz is deeper as we go deeper into the etymology of the zodiac. The term zodiac means "circle of animals," which in its term derives from Latin "Zodiacus" and Greek. The Greeks inherited their knowledge from the Mesopotamians, who in turn inherited their knowledge from the Sumerians. As we go deeper into AngelGoonz, we now overstand that all of this animal and relation to the zodiac temple in Egypt, the temple of Dendera. The Dendera zodiac is an ancient base-relief temple ceiling carved with mysterious symbols of stars and planets. During the Napoleonic Egypt Campaign (1798-1801), French scientists discovered the zodiac in the ceiling of the small chapel atop a temple outside the town of Dendera, near Thebes. Note: Thebes is a replica of Chiraz in ancient times, with half-animals, half-humans, and hippos carrying knives—another topic as we dig deeper into AngelGoonz.

Mother Earth, the Big Mama"of it all, is imperative to note. The dog is the symbol of loyalty. The hippo is Big Mama; she doesn't have the knife but a "SA" Egyptian SA. This emulates the hieroglyphics that write "S," which means protection to the wearer, whether in life or death. The piece was found in the same tomb with a separate bead wood box. If you want to know more as we go deeper in search of overstanding, search "BA," the symbol of eternal life carried by the bird. BA is represented as a human head that leaves the body when a person dies, the face of the exact likeness of the deceased person. AKI is the spirit of RA, which encapsulates the concept of light in the transfigured spirit of a person that becomes one with light after death.

Waking up to light after you leave the physical body is like Anna, Queen of Heaven and Earth, carrying the same symbol. Her feet are an owl, the symbol of the owl. The bird spirit, the blood from the left to the right, rules standing on two lions, utilizing the power of the owl as a totem to carry on through the dream realm. This is Black woman magic, Black girl magic. Standing on the zodiac sign of Leo, this is how they keep all the evil going, antagonizing to nature. All of this Black war on Black America is only to prevent the...

Coalition of black groups to keep blacks from awakening to the pure truth of it all because, as I stress, the truth doesn't need any help to prevent the rise of the black messiah who will educate people of all races about the real truth and nothing but the truth, so help us God in

Heaven, not God in Hell. Preventing a black coalition that could unify and electrify black nationalist positive movements from gaining responsibility by illegally and intentionally discrediting the positive blessings from these black groups who simply wanted and want to educate and learn by teaching and empowering our black youth. Changing the wicked narrative brought on by a blind eye to white supremacy over blood and money, diamonds, and oil, all by blood from Babylon to the United Snakes of America, killing all progress of blacks, robbing them of the complete knowledge of self is the worst of the worst.

The Black Panther Party started the free breakfast and lunch programs, and they hated that so much because if you can feed a people, you can lead a people into positivity. But instead, white supremacy made up lies and murdered as many Black Panthers for nothing other than trying to improve the black community. The same black community the government helped corrupt through brainwashing and religion. We tie all this together, and we see why they discredited the street kings through "tricknology," and black unification scares the hell out of them. But I truthfully don't know why. As much hell as they have and are causing all over the Earth, causing hurt and putting people in the dirt, robbing other people's nations of their natural resources, they hate black unity and will kill and die to continue in their love for blood and blood money because, as my favorite rapper Young Dolph says, "The money got blood all on it." They aim to prevent the long-term growth of black people in the name of Jesus, and most people don't know that there are two "Jesus Christs." One for us, the good one, and the one that they made to suit their needs and to justify their treatment of us blacks in America, especially the youth.

Go google the FBI confession from a dying agent and put it all together, and you'll see that it all started when the pope sent Spain over here. The pope allowed Spain first rights under the discoveries of the white man's burdens. When they came over here, we blacks were fighting the Spaniards. All our people were starting to accumulate in the Gulf of Mexico and the surrounding lands. If you don't believe me, then go look up the American Native American migrating path to Florida. When the French did come to the fort of New Orleans, we were migrating from all over the land to Florida. People get it twisted about Trump and Florida, but for the sake of AngelGo-onz, that's a whole other topic or book. We were trading with them from Florida to New Orleans passage. By way, change the "F" to a "P," and now it's Port of New Orleans.

Before Columbus ever came, this is where everyone had to come "check-in." In 1803, for 15 million dollars, the French mulattoes turned tail and ran. The French, funny, funny, funny Moors, the French lost the battle with the Haitians. This is what made them have to leave Spanish territory in 1803. The Spanish Armada signed in France. Why? According to the Northwest Trading Company, the conquistadors were fighting in Florida and Mexico, fighting for dominance over our land. Royal Moorish Trading Company, 1800.

However, examining AngelGoonz, we go deeper, praying for family protection. We must overstand the Oreo cookie, overstanding that men who argue like women only bring out the pure bitch in them, especially the backdooring and the setup artistry used in killings, black on black. In terms of digging into the Willie Lynch letters, instead of talking to the woman and developing a greater overstanding of all that is going on in order to make it all make sense, booty lickers and backstabbers with low self-esteem argue with the woman, and she is the one who carried them and us all for not only nine months but the whole damn time throughout humanity.

She is our helpmate, so don't hate, appreciate, mate. They just need to stop acting bitchified and treat our women like queens because I promise you, if she doesn't have all the answers we need, she can sure get them quickly from Almighty God. He visits her frequently in the womb and is a caretaker of the womb because it is sacred and holy to Him, who cares for Mother Nature because the womb is God's workshop.

For producing all life, including the "Messiah," when we hold hands in church or the mosque, God is talking to us all the time. Many second guess it, but I don't second guess God because I trust God. All I desire is the truth. Don't lie to yourself by continuing to believe all the lies of the blind leading the blind only for wealth. Give yourself the right answer, and the reason will appear.

Holding hands in church, the palms' "chakras" require holding hands properly to get the maximum effects of the chakras' alignment. The fingers should be interlocked, not hands closed together. The reason we interlock the fingers is that we have what are called "meridians" at each fingertip and on the back of the hands. These correspond to each other. The chakras in your palms mean, beloved, if you put your two hands together and lock them, "and not like they taught you to pray in church with fingers open extended up, no." They must be interlocked. That's the "proper technique." Notice the fingertips touch the back of your hands. These are the "meridians to meridians" connections. Are you following me?

Okay, now let's go ahead and get "deep" into it. In the palm of your hands is a chakra, which is an open "channel." When we do that position, women can then move energy, and whatever it may be, let it be. Remember, God said, "Be," and it was. When God says, "Be," whatever it is, it is easy for God. God simply says, "Be" to a thing, and whatever it is that God said "Be" to simply "be," and it is. Quit worrying about the "he" because the "he" created "her." Mother Nature doesn't have a knife in her feet or hands. She only has a heart in her hands of pure love, worthy to be respected and loved. She is the mother to all. She is the woman, the giver of life that God produces through her for His glorification. No one can get to heaven without the agency of a woman, but many will go to hell with the agency of the most powerful entity on earth, "against God disguised as Christ in a robe of white supremacy."

Let it be of God that we go after the heart of God in heaven and create a heaven on earth for ourselves. Set ourselves in heaven at once and be not malicious because it will come back sevenfold. Be as positive in prayer. Good prayers are the "key." It's all about seeking the God within and replacing the god without. Love outward, Satan, and replace him with God in heaven because ultimately what we are dealing with is a false god, a form of godliness mixed with "tricknology," glitter, and play. Evil made "fair-seeming," and they have been "crossing" everybody out ever since. So what we're seeking is something more wholesome, more meaningful, and most of all, more "soulfulness" to keep us closest to God in heaven because, in the eyesight of God, growing within to shine outward completely without doubt in your first mind.

We must not leave this part of our journey without looking at the sick behavior and the "disease" of the evilness of raping Black men ("buck jumping"), raping Black women, and raping Black children to instill fear. Fear never leaves a child's memory and is an evil controlling mechanism. Those committing these acts claim personal property rights given by Satan under white supremacy—of slave owners, past and present, modern-day and Hollywood. They have the power to attack Black people whenever they decide. Freddy Krueger only had power and only has power over those who are asleep, even those who are "Oreo cookies"—Black people who choose to remain asleep, letting their boss pop them on the ass with a corny white joke, and they do nothing but laugh. However, if their own brother, who looks like them, accidentally steps on their shoes, they will kill him without a second thought.

On top of all this evilness done to us and our people by our oppressors, including the poisoning of our food, air, and water, the real killing part is that so-called Negroes want to pay attention to all the bullshit instead of the real issues. Even the people publishing this book might run away from these facts and want to call it racist because they want to turn the other cheek and not deal with the real cancer in the world: white supremacy and greed from Satan's gangsters who oppose the truth and hide it with continuous lies and bullshit excuses. If they don't publish this book because of secrecy and being in bed with Satan, they are literally poisoning Black children and babies.

Way before Black parents and Black babies were even born, there was already a plan to destroy us before we even had a chance. Many rappers are the biggest sellouts because artificial intelligence and digital currency are part of the plot. The biggest war is economic; not all wars are fought with bullets and bombs. Start buying gold and silver. That's really why they killed Gaddafi, allegedly because he didn't want to accept the American dollar or any paper money. Gaddafi wanted America to purchase his oil with gold, but the problem with that is, as I said, there isn't any gold at Fort Knox.

So when our children are born, they're born to fail by a system that claims Christianity, but America's actions only prove that they are Satan's gangsters. We don't know what to expect from them, especially with giving babies Similac types of milk—something they made similar to synthetic milk poison—and taking God out of schools only puts Satan in the schools. This only hurts the child, poisoning the baby with a similar guinea pig milk to try out on Black babies because their own biological bodies lack melanin sufficient enough to sustain their own white babies, lacking melanin to fight disease, sun cancer, etc. This poison is passed down directly through the mitochondrial DNA to the Black child, the offspring of the Black nation of people as a whole race. Damn, what an evil shit storm. Then, corrupting the full functionality of the generation, included with the Willie Lynch letters, damn, they never expected us to have a fighting chance at nothing but hell, which they created and continue to create.

The real color that matters may be green, the color of money, but by the way of all the modern-day lynchings of Blacks, anybody who says they're not worried about color between Black and white is delusional and an Oreo cookie. If you're Black and feel that way, all I can say is when the chickens you talk about don't matter come home to roost, don't call on any help. Call on those who say color doesn't matter. When that color that doesn't matter kills your mother, father, daughter, family, or whatever happens once they come home to roost, please keep that same energy and live in your own delusions. But don't push it on those who desire to break free from bondage and praise God in Heaven only. Because Satan's got some gangsters, but God's got some goons—angel goons—from A to Z. ANGELGOONZ

BY MINISTER MELVIN"A.P.D. T.A. ....ANGELGOONZ

ANGELGOONZ

Let us intensify our efforts as we go deeper into Angelgoonz. We, the people seeking true freedom, justice, and equality on our journey, must also intensify our prayers, keep an untroubled spirit, put our feet on the green grass in the soil, and remember that our enemies can always trick us, but our so-called friends can kill us quicker. Taking all of this into prayer and giving it all to God, the universe will respond. However you pray, let's get into the "electrical" storms of alkaline spring water and distilled water. We have different types of water, all of which are apparently poisoned and allegedly killing people by "zipcode." Different types of water, but we must keep in mind that "gold water" is something we must start drinking when we can afford it. It's the next big market if people pay attention, and that's something they don't want you to really pay too much attention to. Most of it is in the cerebral spinal fluid, but they know all this because they have their own water, air, and pork diabetes disease method to enhance the death experience of the people they reluctantly fear due to their own personal guilt, which they care absolutely nothing about. Faults are always copied, and they don't become faults anymore; they become evilness in a way of life through the pain you inflict on the poor. The evil that has been done, the dirtiest of the dirtiest, is the Blacks, so-called "Negros," ever in history. The worst was ever done to a people. Complete before being tampered with is a complete disaster and often looked over because of the guilt of racism through forced slavery.

So as we go to prayer, let us pray with forgiveness but never be too perceiving because their tricks are deceiving. Spells are cast, so be careful who you're praying to because Satan blesses too. But I'd rather be what everyone thinks is poor than be rich with a lot of pain, trouble, and hate from the inside out. The gold water helps us through our "electrical" systems as we pray with open-mindedness. It is a suspension of sub-micron nanoparticles (AuNPs) suspended with a solvent, most often water. AuNPs have unique optical, electronic, and thermal properties and are being incorporated into a wide variety of technologies, including microscopy, electronics, diagnostics, and therapeutics. As we dig and learn, even diatomic gold and clean water, we must drink good water and bathe in good water before prayer. Now, the new age of Aquarius is here, something that everyone said didn't exist or start yet. But it started in 2012; the Mayan calendar was never changed from the closing of the age. When we read Edgar Cayce, he tells us that around the years 2012 to 2019, a great teacher was going to come on the scene and begin teaching the world. You can also find the same prophecy if you follow Nostradamus. They know the closing of the age is coming. Nostradamus gave the same prophecy predicting Vladimir Putin, lord of the worlds. Be careful; either way, they will always appear contrary and opposite to the facts of the Book of Revelation. The Bible clearly states the lord of the worlds has hair of wool and skin of bronze.

This is all essential to understand: there are three "oracles," and these three oracles have had the same exact prophecy for over 2000 years. For all three of them to have covered God in thought and under a 500-year period is significant. So, a lot of Oreo cookies and KKK skeptics or Bible thumpers, the only reason they can all agree on the above-mentioned prophecy is that it's mentioned in the Book of Revelation. But they leave out the facts, all the facts concerning the true race or color, as they like to use, as they cover up all facts of anything good about the Black race to make the whole world hate and not love us as a people. We have been taught to hate and not love ourselves. The permission of blood money through low vibrational frequency music promotes rituals, though most rappers and people forget that in spiritual, there is the word ritual. Spells are being cast over our young entrepreneurs in the music industry to chase the bag, promoting killing your own in the name of God. But which God? The churches go along to get along with the lies they know are lies because they mislead the masses of the people on the basis of the bag also. We spend all our time eating poison in the name of Jesus. We pay taxes in the name of Jesus. We follow the pastor who has to give an account on our behalf in the name of Jesus, so they teach. But when we have members in the church that want to borrow money from the church to start a business, to truly seek out not the American dream but the God-given dreams of goals and aspirations, the church says no. That's a problem that nobody wants to talk about or prophesy about because many of these churches are getting big government kickbacks.

But it all goes back to the truth and facts purely concerning the Book of Revelation. The fact that it mentions the Pale Horse—who knows what that is? A lot of these Oreo cookies and backstabbers of the worst kind are Black as the ace of spades, and they purely exemplify a white K. Don't talk to me about white people, because I know some white people who are more Black than Black people who are Black for real. Their exemplifications exemplify what it is to be Christlike for real. But that will never stop me from bringing to the forefront, speaking truth to power concerning white privilege and the mistreatment of Blacks by Blacks taught by whites. Just go visit the Willie Lynch letters. The white mother whore America, Babylon, the once-great city or nation, has fallen and will continue to fall if she doesn't do the right thing by her slaves. Yes, slaves. Modern-day slavery exists on two points: prison (13th Amendment) and the Willie Lynch letters (slavery of the mind, the worst kind).

Now look, beloved, I feel the need to go on ahead and get deep into it. The Bible, the King James version, was allegedly a book of demons. The book asserts James' full belief in witchcraft. Yes, brothers and sisters in Christ, in God, in Muhammad—they believe in it and practice it. But they didn't and don't want you to. Why? The book of demonology is the fact that demons are not all what they told you they were. But he sold out the "true" Moorish people for a seat at the throne. We must remember to control our own minds or someone else will control it. King James stole all of our secrets of the Bible, and when I say "our secrets," I'm not talking about Blacks; I'm talking about all of us as a world of people with the ultimate goal of white supremacy worship on Earth. Anyone who denies that is the exemplification of a real devil. I don't give a damn what color you are; the truth doesn't need any help until it has been tampered with. And nobody on Earth has been more tampered with than the Black man, the Black race, his Black race that everyone desires to own. When they own your mind, they also own you. So as King James stole all of the original texts, then flipped them upside down and inside out, "Black people"—because the Bible is full of Black people but pastors and ministers fail to teach Blacks where they are in the Bible—we are there, and the Anunnaki are there also, assisting white supremacy all the way with the dark side of Satan and his real demons of the mind, body, and soul, all of which white supremacy wants to control. I mean, they want it all. So when they turned the Bible inside out and upside down, they shook up the very foundation of God's truth and distorted it to fit their narrative of white supremacy. You have to admit it's white supremacy because he and the Pope ordered all original African history of Black excellence to be torn down. No matter how significant and great, tear it down and rebrand it as white. Destroy all remembrance except what they want to keep, steal it and bring it to Rome, England, and everywhere else. They robbed us of everything and called it biblical fact. Also, Constantine had already cast the Moors out in 325 AD and had a group of priests assemble the Bible. All King James did was commission the scholars of the day to render it from Latin. It had become a Septuagint Greek Old Testament. Septuagint is the earliest Greek translation from the Hebrew Bible. It includes several books beyond those contained in the Masoretic text of the Hebrew Bible because the Hebrew version has three divisions: the

Torah (Law), the Nevi'im (Prophets), and the Ketuvim (Writings). The Septuagint, on the other hand, has four: Law, History, Poetry, and Prophets. Many are grouped together in the Septuagint.

We need all the prayers of good as we unravel Satan's gangsters. God in heaven has some goons from A to Z. ANGELGOONZ

BY MINISTER MELVIN A.P.D.T.A. ANGELGOONZ

The Hebrew and Greek council of Nicaea, first overseen by Emperor Constantine, was convened to resolve the controversy within the church. But they were "melanated" like me and you. We have to understand that the enemy is working after HIV-1, HIV-2, HIV-3, and everything to kill the Black race, enough to change the dynamics of procreation of the Black race and the Black birth rate, which they "all fear" to this very day. They were worried about us back then before they conquered us and robbed us of everything. Yet, their numbers are dwindling, and they are really worried. But I don't get it because white and Black is now a way of life. So was it always about race? Color? Or evilness from the dark side of "white supremacy"? Satan's gangsters love to rule this world and aren't going to truly rule anything but hell. They think because God in heaven will have Angelgoonz overseeing hell, no one, no devils, or Oreos will escape. Who should have just loved who God in heaven made them the color they are? Black. And as far as white people go, and everybody else, they all love their so-called "race." Only Black people have been taught self-hate by a hateful teaching by Oreo cookies and the Willie Lynch people. Now, was Willie Lynch "white" or was Willie Lynch "Black"? I don't know, maybe an Oreo. Either way, according to the mystic teachings, the secret teachings of all ages of all times, all this matters because it affects us all to this day.

Manly P. Hall is a good place to start to develop your own reasoning and understanding, or overstanding if you wish to continue to be under it all, go ahead. But Manly P. Hall is a good place to start with over 150 volumes on the history of the ages. Sift through his words to uncover the facts of the truth to get on track. "Isis Unveiled" is another one. We have to look at tribal structures, structure a corporation; all of the "bearded" is the structure to set up the tribes. We must assess the skill set of people involved, and then we will understand what to make them a minister of. Now, I ask, we must ask whenever encountered: 1. Who are you? 2. What do you want? 3. Where are we going?

Well, the Emerald Tablets and it all come out as to how you or these questions are answered. You know it is demonology with a twist. Let's say someone is studying "demonology" to become rich and successful. It works because all a demon is, is a "thought form" from an egregore that was created a long time ago by priests to teach us how to access higher consciousness. Each one of these demons must be adequately put back on whatever shelf you got them from when you're done with them. That's why there's absolutely nothing wrong with hoodoo or voodoo. As a matter of fact, when you do practice correctly, a good book for beginners to at least learn more about the facts is a book by the awesome Queen "Alisha J. Brown." When you don't practice correctly, the spirits will let you know because they come out in the next generation. If we're not good, then all of the evil thereof, the evil that we are seeing depicted every day from the worst of evils, will come out because of your praying for bad. When you don't do good, that's all we're doing. When we are not doing good deeds through and through, then we are praying for bad, praying for evil. The very evil we pray to avoid is a life "void," and soon paranoid bad will come through to our next generation, and everybody will blame them with good reason. Exodus 20:5 says the sins of the "father" will be passed down to the next generation. Through that next generation, they have to blame you because there is no one else to blame. They can't blame fathers, so God makes it clear that the sins will be passed down whether we like it or not. But what's imperative to note here is that God judges, and we must be very careful to let God do just what he is doing. All we have to do is just let Mother Nature handle it all for us because trusting Satan to do the right thing is just like asking hell to freeze over, and that's just not going to happen. The enemy is not worried about hell because it was an addition added to the Bible in the 2nd century. So Babylon feels she is exempt, so we must be careful not to blame them ourselves when we already know they know. But when they continue to act like God is mocked, they will soon see that everything goes back into its originality. Yacub is over with; the Anunnaki will not be able to assist Jacob in any evil way as before. Galactic law prevents it. God in heaven is still in control. He's just so merciful, and they take advantage of him, so they think. But soon they will be made to know once the great mother whore America, Babylon, Babylon loses everything because of thievery, robbery, death, and greed to feed their lust for blood and money. Ancestral sins are in the...

Hands of God in heaven remember, God in heaven can and will handle everything supremely and adequately. Never forget the real enemy that starts it all, and we must always stick closely to those who care most for and about "reform" to the good of man and "the good of mankind." Let God in heaven have His supreme "say" and supreme "way." "Not our will, but His will." So all of this is hoodoo, and not using it correctly, them "hoodoo" and "voodoo" correctly, makes them mad. (The spirits) and they get upset when you're not using them correctly for good.

This is why we have to clean up the family tree so that those who are working righteousness and desiring hard to be with God in heaven, and be Godly, can learn and be Godly accepted by God in heaven for God in heaven. And us. Remember, we have to be ready and willing to sincerely ask those three questions to be able to put them in check. We also have three friends that we have to always be mindful of: our feelings, our thoughts, and our opinions. Because ultimately we have God, demons, and greed, and all feelings, no matter what they are, they have to all add up to our feelings, thoughts, and opinions in accordance with the Creator of it all concerning life. The same energy that goes into creating a personality by opening the energy of the demon is, in itself, a demonstration of the "mind" that has been taken over by "mankind," which is sort of like opening up "apps" to the psyche. Thus, since Satan's got some gangsters...

GOD GOT SOME "GOONZ" "THUS" "ANGELGOONZ"

By MINSTER"MELVIN "A"P"D"T"A"

. . .

ANGELGOONZ Minister Melvin Mahamad A.P.D.T.A.

The human "Psyche" that was written along time ago dear beloved reader if you are beloved?????

Hands of God in heaven remember, God in heaven can and will handle everything supremely and adequately. Never forget the real enemy that starts it all, and we must always stick closely to those who care most for and about "reform" to the good of man and "the good of mankind." Let God in heaven have His supreme "say" and supreme "way." "Not our will, but His will." So all of this is hoodoo, and not using it correctly, them "hoodoo" and "voodoo" correctly, makes them mad. (The spirits) and they get upset when you're not using them correctly for good.

This is why we have to clean up the family tree so that those who are working righteousness and desiring hard to be with God in heaven, and be Godly, can learn and be Godly accepted by God in heaven for God in heaven. And us. Remember, we have to be ready and willing to sincerely ask those three questions to be able to put them in check. We also have three friends that we have to always be mindful of: our feelings, our thoughts, and our opinions. Because ultimately we have God, demons, and greed, and all feelings, no matter what they are, they have to all add up to our feelings, thoughts, and opinions in accordance with the Creator of it all concerning life. The same energy that goes into creating a personality by opening the energy of the demon is, in itself, a demonstration of the "mind" that has been taken over by "mankind," which is sort of like opening up "apps" to the psyche. Thus, since Satan's got some gangsters?

The hands of God in heaven are above the grasp of those crawling on the earth. Self-hate is a learned behavior, and we must function on a high vibrational frequency, becoming "one" with the Almighty Creator, God in heaven. As people who understand the mind and control on a high level of spirituality, we must avoid "wine spirits or drugs." Those are the wrong kind of spirits to conjure in this era. Remember the poison of chemically modified food, poisoning of the water, poisoning, and pollution of the ozone layer in the air we breathe. The color of money is real and outweighs the treatment of evil in the name of the cross. All this closes up the pineal gland and poisons the minds of the next generation—physically, mentally, and more importantly, spiritually—because so much pain is being inflicted under what is supposed to be "holy," the "cross." They have been crossing out all poor and oppressed people for the benefit of greed, and soul selling is at an all-time high. Only God in heaven can fix this, only God can save us through Mother Nature, which they are and have been also "tampering" with, playing God to keep us all in the dark.

God is saving people every day, putting us on the straight path. Those three questions I asked earlier: 1. Who are you? 2. What do you want? 3. Where are you going? When we practice what God is teaching us, whoever tries to bring us harm—when we ask those three questions, God will reveal and "decimate" their evil intentions immediately, as long as we are on "code" with the Creator. Asking these questions helps put us on code and in alignment with God and His Angelgoonz in heaven and on earth. It puts them on notice that we belong to God in heaven and that we are the wrong ones to "mess with." A good manual to get is called *The Magic Circle*; it will open up a lot of information needed to truly grow.

I must stress, and I can't stress it enough, that Dr. Claud Anderson makes things crystal clear in *PowerNomics*. I believe in his teachings to awaken a sleeping generation. Dr. Claud Anderson is an "Angelgoon" on earth, sent by the Creator. A prophet is never accepted in his own "hometown" or "home." No, I'm not saying Dr. Claud Anderson is a prophet; I'm simply stating the facts from the Creator, God in heaven. So God has taught me, and play with me or God if you want to. But I warn you, my God is "not mocked." Information to grow a good flock is also in the book by YAJ NOMOLOS. Women should start there. Keep in mind the setting up of a "covenant" tribe of good family morals and good moral tribes in the family. NOMOLOS is "Solomon" spelled backward, and the book for setting up ceremonies is for womanhood. That's why they were murdering witches, burning them at the stake, because these were indeed the wise "matriarchs" actually able to access and use the power of nature to originally keep the imposters off the land. The original inhabitants they label as Indians. And while I'm at it, let me ask a question: Who do you all think was fighting to keep the imposters off our land? So-called cowboys in all the western movies? It wasn't.

They called them $5 Indians; it was us, the Blacks, the real Native Americans. They just stole it all and replaced us. I got to protect us and our heritage. The Bible teaches that, but God teaches it better when He sends "Angelgoonz" to play His "tune." The tune of hip-hop is as phony as Obama acting like he was really elected by us, then did nothing while white police officers murdered Blacks at an all-time high. Obama was selected, not elected, and he did nothing for Black people besides bridging the gap and replacing rap music masculinity with feminism and gay rights to back it up. Whenever we talk about the past, we see the effects in the future. Whenever they found women teaching truth from God, the enemy struck the woman, using money to make the lie look like the truth. This led to rituals being conducted more in secret.

To be a good person, cleaned up, is the key. Our children should only have to worry about learning how to invest money properly. The man and woman should use their minds together to bring everything into fruition. The enemy, afraid of this, labels Black children with ADHD and white children with ADHD, fearing they might solve our race problems. Everyone is afraid to confront the truth because they are guilty. They fear the awakening of the Black Messiah, who the Bible says will come from his own people with the help of a white ally.

All of this is due to our enemies knocking us over the head. What is the 64-dollar question? 64 years vanished from history. Raping of our women, raping of our men (literally, they call it buck breaking), and the raping of our children—all of this is passed down through mitochondrial DNA, all the pain of the Blacks through the Black woman who has been there through it all. She sticks with her man, no matter what, because she understands, but still plays her part. Yet, all we have been taught to do is disrespect her in rap music, casting spells of bitches and hoes. Their favorite word is "on God," but I ask, "which God?"

The raping of our people was done in front of the whole tribe or town, not by gangsters in government, and especially not in their courts. All courts are a result of Roman Christianity rule, with the Pope and Europe. Europe doesn't have a rope in it for no reason, and the Pope doesn't rhyme with rope for no reason. In today's society, the modern-day Queen allegedly passed, but we believe she has been dead longer than announced, in order for the Pope to cash in his receipts for Satan. Allegedly, it is believed. Since Satan's got gangsters, God has some too, from "A" to "Z"—"Angelgoonz." By Minister Melvin A.P.D. TA.

It's all ironically coming together, and believe it or not, that's okay. The fact of the real matter is that they are doing all this resistance and evil to us more and more every day because of the guilt associated with the evil that they have and have continued to do under the veil of "Christianity." The children of them are crying out because they don't want to continue living and "functioning" under such hypocrisy any longer. They are tired of all the lies associated with keeping our stolen legacies, histories, and great accomplishments hidden. They want to be real and genuine as a race without deceit, contempt, and wickedness mixed with Satanism. They want out, so they are acting out in a major way. Mass shootings are up in their communities, and interestingly enough, they blame it on bullying. Yeah, bullying alright, in reverse. They are waiting on all the evil, and according to God in heaven and the Black Knight Satellite, we are waiting too.

As they create and continue to create emergencies, they call in what they call "FEMA," in which they have a group of "Matriarchs," sisters from all communities across the land with experience in various fields. One might be in charge of animal rescue, another disaster relief, a third in charge of feeding all the children and elderly in the communities, and another with expertise in higher consciousness and spirituality. What they possess is what we need to be successful, and we will be because of He in heaven. God in heaven is not mocked. Satan is by his own kind. That's how and why they cancel each other out and don't even know it. Oh, they do know it, but they don't help. In their eyes, they are giving it and us one hell of a hellish life before they get up out of here. They are counting on science big time to save and aid them, but what they forgot to keep hold of is God is science, and you can't beat God in heaven at His own game.

As I was saying, Angelgoonz and even the military—it goes on and on. We need the woman because they were, after all, doing exceptionally well with the recovery of soldiers and the communities, better than the VA. Veterans Affairs is going to be shifted over to that new organization that's going to be heavily funded. They understand that it's run by veterans who over-stand, not understand under any white supremacy from Rome. Quit telling us to go home because we were already here. Why don't they go home? They think they ain't, but we don't care where they go. But God in heaven says they're going somewhere. They can stay here with the continuation of all this evil, calling it holy, knowing it's unholy. Overstanding this struggle is real, it's eventually going to die off because with us in our proper place, on and in our proper land, it's plain and simple.

Besides, the only reason God wouldn't destroy America to begin with for all her sins against us is because we are still here. We believe we can all get along and live well— just do the right thing by us because God in heaven is not mocked. Before they came over here, we didn't have dirty wars of evilness tied deeply to Satan. They brought that with them from England, Europe, Rome, etc. But we will have none of that mess, all over greed and laziness mixed with their hunger for slaves on a more modern-day level. They love evil just like their father Satan, that's why they do what they do with all the hating. And it's crazy because they hate and turn you with a smile as a crocodile.

But for right now, we do have warriors that have suffered and fought in these wars. Now we're going to be using them with boots on the ground to help our communities. We need to reorganize as we redistribute the wealth. They bring in new recruits from all these government agencies that have been defunct for so many years—3 or 4, etc. but still using the templates for training to maximize the use of the experience of aged ones who are leaving. We must take what we need from the old system, and there ain't a damn thing they can do about it because God in heaven is tired, and everything is getting ready to come to a head because He, God in heaven, is the head.

God's system of righteousness will teach us, from the learned—yes, Lord—from the best in the field with the best intentions. We are ready to always stay ready to keep from getting ready. To do the best, we must give our best, and we will pass this test. Our melanin says so as far as the sun is concerned. We're not worried at all to give our people, the oppressed by imposed stress on both white and Black, the American dream, especially after coming from kings and queens. They broke every treaty, and in case you're wondering who the real so-called Indians...

· · ·

Are you aware of how white supremacy tells its vision on the silver screen, with "red" Indians fighting white supremacy through white supremacy? Those weren't 5-dollar Indians they were fighting in the cowboy films. That was us, the Blacks, who were already here making treaties with these people who were evil-minded from the jump. We were too trusting and forgiving. We didn't believe they could be so evil. Talking about raping white women and children? We never did that. They simply told the stories in reverse on television, and they have been telling that same old sad story ever since. Even with Emmett Till, he never did anything to that white woman. White supremacy is real, and Satan's got some gangsters. Well, God's got some goonz.

White supremacy has been... us to become great again because it means love and true peace will return for good. And Satan doesn't want that. He would rather try and blow up the whole world before he sees us return to our former glory with God in heaven. Well, Satan's got some gangsters. God's got some goonz.

From "A" to "Z"—Angelgoonz, by Minister Melvin A.P.D.T.A.,

You know, "Beloved," I just received "ANGELGOONZ" to let you know that while we are working on transformation in terms of claiming what's rightfully ours, we must remember that millions of us were already here in the Americas. To keep us prepared, we must recognize that the opposition and open enemy is not only represented by the pale horse in Revelation but also by the Mother Whore, who doesn't leave Babylon the Great. Once a great nation adorned in gold, diamonds, and more, it exploited so-called Black people, robbing us while others reap the benefits of our suffering. The enemy is literally "hell-bent" on continuing to take what rightfully belongs to us, hoping to achieve evil solidarity by stealing from us and giving it to everyone else, despite the holy name of Jesus.

In the end, everything will turn against this entity, and the Whore—America—will face its downfall as the dollar continuously declines. To stay ready, we must be prepared and vigilant, as the enemy remains unchanged. The opposition includes not only those who openly oppress but also those who pretend to be allies while sabotaging us from within. They operate on a very low frequency, and their goal is to destroy what God is giving back to us.

It's crucial to understand that God is revealing those who are generationally connected to the ones who betrayed us. Many who sold us into slavery were those who looked like us, and those enslaved were taken from

Africa under brutal conditions. However, many of us were already here in the Americas long before the arrival of the so-called slave masters. The Annunaki, the schemes, and the pale white horse are all real. The truth is that we had been coming and going from the Americas on our own accord long before the slave trade.

The blue-eyed beast is mentioned in both the Bible and the Quran, and it's essential to recognize that the actions taken against us were devilish. Christianity was used as a tool of control, and the letter "J" was invented later to fit their narrative. This is not a message of hate but of truth. The truth is painful, but it's necessary for awakening. The lies taught to us in schools were meant to keep us asleep and confused.

It's time to confront the truth, develop clear and godly strategies, and focus on finding ways to succeed—not sin. The deception against us has been vast, and America has continually covered it up, pretending to be holy while exposing us to further suffering. The teaching of hatred towards Africans to justify exploitation is not aligned with Christ or God in heaven; it is the work of the devil. The blue-eyed men who perpetrated these acts have hidden their hands while attacking us.

Furthermore, they have used drugs like crack and meth to destroy both Black and poor white communities, creating a cycle of addiction and suffering. They exploit and manipulate these communities, ensuring that many do not survive. It is also important to note that not all white people are the same, and there are allies who stand against these injustices.

We must remain vigilant and continue to seek the truth and justice, as God in heaven will ultimately prevail over these evils.

We have more "Oreo-Cookies" among us than there are white people. Some white individuals are more supportive of us than those who look like us but act contrary to our interests. The "Oreo-Cookie" type is particularly harmful because they appear to be one of us but often work against us.

As we continue to explore the concept of "AngelGoonZ," let's not forget that while many of our ancestors came by way of the transatlantic slave trade, the story we were told was distorted. Yes, people were brought over on slave ships, but the truth has been manipulated. I believe I am one of those who was lost but found, cleaned up by God, much like many of us in the ghettos are transformed by the teachings of the Nation of Islam. The Nation has done a tremendous job of uplifting and reforming those whom the enemy sought to destroy.

The truth is that there are two interpretations of Jesus: the one they know and the real one. Through the teachings of truth, we shall be free. The Most Honorable Minister Louis Farrakhan has always been sent from God in Heaven to help us. However, America rejects this help from a Black man because it forces her to confront her guilt. Minister Farrakhan has even offered to sit down and have a dialogue, but the truth will always prevail.

The Jews, if truthful, would acknowledge the secret relationship between Blacks and Jews, which would require them to examine their own roles in this dynamic. The goal of keeping the foot on the necks of Black people—those who resemble the biblical description of God with hair of wool and skin of bronze—is rooted in evil. The Bible speaks of "burnt feet," not "olive skin," so go read it for yourself.

My mother always said to "read between the lines," not just "dangle" between them. Even scientists are now confirming much of what the Honorable Elijah Muhammad spoke about concerning science and the earth. Life began in Africa, and this is not a message of hate but of truth. The real hate is in not teaching pure truth.

Dr. Sebi, a holistic doctor, championed natural healing and was opposed by big pharma. His mysterious death has been attributed by some to population control and MKUltra experiments. They often target Black individuals for such experiments because we are considered the first-born of God, and the truth is where all the answers lie.

Everything begins in Africa, as it is the cradle of humanity. Satan has some gangsters, but God has some goons —"AngelGoonZ"—by Minister Melvin A.P.D.T.A.

GOD HAS SOME GOONZ "ANGELGOONZ" BY MINISTER"MELVIN"A.P.D. TA.

ANGELGOONZ

As we continue to delve deeper into "AngelGoonZ," beginning with the letter "A" and ending with "S" for Satan, we recognize that his end is imminent. The Almighty God will conclude the 6,000-year rule of Satan, who seeks to take as many souls to hell with him. The last letter of the alphabet, "Z," signifies the end of this era.

Our exploration of the Annunaki and their oath reveals a deep-seated solidarity built into their legacy. This solidarity has been passed down through generations. Historically, while the pale white horse symbolizes evil, this solidarity was ingrained in those who once lived in

Europe's caves and hillsides. They vowed, with the help of evil, to place animals above human life, particularly prioritizing the dog—an animal whose importance they exaggerated to serve their purposes.

The Annunaki, under their oath, were not supposed to create Homo sapiens capable of procreation beyond specific restrictions. This oath, however, was broken by Enki, who engaged in reproduction contrary to these guidelines. Genesis 6:2 in the Bible mentions that the "Sons of God" saw that the daughters of men (the Adamites) were fair and took them as wives by force.

It is crucial to understand that these "Sons of God" are not the original Elohim, who are entirely distinct from Satan's gangsters. The "Sons of God" kidnapped and made the daughters of Adamites their wives. This incident is related to the Nephilim, who are described as giants or mighty men of renown. The term "Nephilim" means "those who fell" or "giants," implying they were significant and powerful beings.

Verse 3 of Genesis states that God's spirit would not strive with man forever because man is flesh, and flesh is weak. God's presence would be limited to 120 years. In verse 4, it mentions the Nephilim—giants or ancient ones who lived on Earth. The term "children" in this context is italicized, indicating it was not part of the original Hebrew text. Instead, it means that mighty men or renowned figures emerged from these unions.

Enki's breach of the oath involved granting these beings (referred to as "lulu") the ability to reproduce. Enki, being half reptilian and half Annunaki, passed on these traits to the lulu. The lulus were taught about sexual reproduction and sexual arousal, aligning with teachings from Hindu traditions like Kama Sutra, which studied love and sex.

The reptilian aspect of Enki and his background connects to the Draco or Draconian entities. These entities, sometimes associated with the Bermuda Triangle and Atlantis, have been linked to various myths and legends. This mixture of origins and the influence of these beings adds complexity to the historical and spiritual narratives we examine.

Called the "Primitives" or the "Falcons" that live in the sea, were from the far star constellation, which is probably where they got "Star Trek" and all the other TV shows telling a vision that was already here to begin with. We need to look no further than the hieroglyphs and refer to Zeta Reticuli. What's more important is that they originated from the planet Aldebaran, but when their planet was destroyed by residents on Earth, others took residence in the "Constellations," Draco, and as mentioned above, Zeta Reticuli. The ones called the Primitive Ones and the others known as the Beast Dragon or "Draco," both were "Constantly" resting with the human race in hopes of then "Breeding" more types of humanoids, cloning, etc., to take over the planet. This led up to revelations in the Bible. Meanwhile, as we all desperately try to live together in America, White and Black is a reality that Satan and his gangsters can't stomach. The fact of the whole matter is that the Messiah is not just coming to save Black people; He's coming to save all by the color of the heart, White people too— everyone who desires to live in peace. The primitives of the Bermuda Triangle, sometimes called Atlantis, is where a lot of discrepancies occur, even to this very day. Well, Satan's got some gangsters; God's got some "GOONZ."

"ANGELGOONZ" from "A" to "Z" By Minister Melvin A. P.D.T.A.

ANGELGOONZ BY MINISTER"MELVIN"

They all were hoping that the inhabitants would accept "Their" ways. After all, being from the water, the Bermuda Triangle, and following old leadership, but all of them were wrong because there was and still is a battle going on between the original people of the earth and the "Problem People." The "OREO COOKIES" is also a wicked "Species" altogether, and the disease is the result of self-hate being spread to the original people.

As we go on, we're really talking about what led up to all the wickedness, which also paves the everlasting way of "GOD" in Heaven to pave the way for AngelGoonZ today. Dr. Claude Anderson is an "ANGELGOON" appointed by "GOD" in Heaven and is the "Catalyst" and the example of what it takes to be a GODLY "ANGELGO-OONZ." Since the beginning, he has been on the front lines fighting to promote pure growth and development in righteousness in the Black communities and as well as others. God is continuing to raise up AngelGoonZ to do the right thing because it's the right thing to do, not the "WHITE" thing to do.

For the good of the planet and for what was coming as a result of all this experimenting, grafting, and "ENKI'S" examples and exemplifications, it is a "Built-in Solidar-ity" that is "CLONED" in "WHITE" Supremacy. It's always been about the "Money," the "GOLD," and all the conductors to help other planets "CONDUCT" and stay grounded according to their needs on various other plan-ets. But all failed, and they chose "EARTH" to dominate, and they have been experimenting and making "Slaves" ever since. White supremacy just simply mastered it—

the "Art" of making "COONZ," "OREOS," and "BAF-FOONZ," which are making it hard for people like all our professors who are great, even the ones without their "Slave Masters' Degree," to do their jobs. But let's make it clear: Dr. Claude Anderson does not have a slave master's degree. He has a heavenly degree of the best kind. The Bible records it like this: "You can tell who GOD'S true people are by their WORKS."

Now let's please get on with it all. AngelGoonZ are inter-dimensional between these two groups of old cloning. It ain't nothing new or intermixing, so white supremacy needs to get over it or completely exist in the metaverse only of some other new so-called afterlife they think they will see. Because it's a way of life now, you all started it. Now "GOD" in Heaven will finish it all with His AngelGoonZ—the ones you see and the ones you don't see.

Now, moving along to the "Reptilians," one set of the "Grafting" and getting rid of things and evaluating the damn planet and taking complete "Wicked Supreme" control with blood to control it. I tell you, it's all about the money. Like one of my favorite rappers, Young Dolph, says, "The money got blood all on it." But moving along, by imprisoning human beings with these space-ships, that's crazily interesting enough in dividing humans literally for breeding. And please, beloved, I don't want you to make no damn "mistakes" about it. We're talking about maybe 3 and 1/2 to 4 feet tall aliens, reptilians in appearance some would say. And since they're having problems completing Satan's orders, maybe that's why white supremacy is in power and poisoning the food, water, and air, not only to kill us but to eliminate the Black and White people who want to get rid of racism and support the offspring of "DIVINE" PEACE between all that GOD in HEAVEN desires.

It took time to get into all this, and it will take time to get out of it. But you can't rush time. You have to "RIDE" TIME. But, them aliens too. Damn... I mean, breeding the genes into the human beings, plus it's the group that its mother "ENKI" came from the world of Zeta. Zeta is the sixth letter in the Greek alphabet, but the letter J wasn't invented until the sixteenth century around the time of the Transatlantic Slave Trade. But we will get back to "J" and "JESUS" and "Christ" another time. The early letter Zeta, however, is the sixth letter of the Greek alphabet. In the system of Greek numbers, it was derived from the Phoenician letter Zayin. The star constellations where it is all exemplified on Earth are only a replica of the cobra, the snake, which really resembles the symbol for the said Zeta, said to be the Zeta Reticulans, with the letter Z being the 7th letter in the Hebrew alphabet. And everybody's trying to forget where all life came from and start their own identity.

. . .

They disassociate themselves from the Africans, the so-called Blacks, and seek to move away from "kinky" hair and dark skin of bronze, opting instead for diluted versions of diluted thoughts through "diluted" grafting to fair skin and fair hair. They suppress and hide the truth of the Lord and the African history of us already being here in these Americas centuries before Columbus. The truth will surface. "GOD" in Heaven is not mocked.

The Reticulans, with the letter Z being the 7th letter in Hebrew, according to biblical tradition, are connected to the Hebrews, who are people of Shem, one of Noah's sons, through Eber, the eponymous ancestor, and Abraham—all of whom are so-called Black. You know, do you all know that using the term "BLACK" used to be considered disrespectful? Anyway, moving along, the term means "defense weapon" as well. However, in the Canaanite or Hebrew name for Cana, ironically connected to the Portuguese password for enslaving Africans and bringing some from Africa as prisoners in chains, it also means "weapon."

Enki, born half reptilian Draco and half Annunaki, was transformed. Enki was preferred on Earth by the Draco dragon reptilians over his brother Enlil. The Draconian men did not like Enlil but loved Enki, which caused most of the conflict between Enki and Enlil. But all the women loved "ENLIL" because he was in control of bringing groups of Annunaki down to Earth. Damn, it was personal, but they wanted to mix their seeds with male Annunaki.

Atlantis is believed to be located off the coast of Bermuda, but it is extremely imperative to note that, as we study the source of the power—the true power of old Atlantis, called the Bermuda Triangle today—the place called Mexico is significant. The sacred double triangle in Mexico becomes the study of Seti, who is David, a Black man. Never mind Hollywood's diluted version of a white David or Jesus; we as Blacks don't care and didn't care what color they were. We just knew and know we needed and need saving. Damn the color. But "somebody" cared enough to hide and erase our true history and that of the Annunaki intermixing.

Anyway, in the Bible, David is referred to with the ascending triangle and the descending triangle in the six-point star. One triangle is in the Bermuda Angels Triangle for "ANGELGOONZ," which is believed also to be on a 32 to 33-degree latitude, connecting from Bermuda to Puerto Rico to Miami, Florida. This inverted triangle points down, while the opposite triangle is the Devil's Triangle in the Pacific Ocean, which he guards well. Ironically, it is also called "The Devil's Sea," reaching as far as the Philippines Sea at the Tropic of Cancer, 32 to 33 degrees latitude. The three points are from northern Philippines, Guam, and the east coast of AngelGoonZ activity in Japan. We will get into that later, but this is the upright triangle. The line that the Tropic of Cancer travels straight around the globe touches all the special spots, including our pyramids in Egypt. And don't forget the Olmec heads in Mexico.

When the others first came to Earth 500,000 years ago, the dragon people and the snake people were already here. They were just unwilling to share or sell a part of the planet; they simply wanted the gold to go back home. The Annunaki called it Paradise, but the dragon people feared that the "ANU" would not accept the "Peaceful" ways of the "Original" People. Satan's got some "gangsters"; GOD'S got some "GOONZ"—"ANGELGOONZ."

FROM"A"TO"Z"

ANGELGOONZ

Though we continue to delve deeper into the Annunaki and their roles, it is essential to understand the symbolism and the impact of the pale white horse in this context. The pale white horse represents a rebellious force against the Creator, "Almighty GOD." Whatever

GOD in Heaven says not to do, the pale white horse endorses. Its role is to make "evil" appear "fair" and "seeming" to man and mankind.

God in Heaven makes it clear not to worship engraven images, yet many people kneel to statues of Peter, John, Mary, and others daily. God says to know the Lord GOD as your GOD, and Jesus instructs to worship the Father only. The pale horse, however, creates confusion by suggesting that Jesus is the only God, even though Jesus himself said, "No one is good but God in Heaven." Complete obedience brings life, while disobedience brings death. The pale horse drives people toward death and destruction by making rebellion against God in Heaven seem appealing.

It is very imperative to understand that when you follow this path, you are engaging with a system built on deceit. These energies have created endless "tunnels" in cooperation with the snake people, leading to what is known as "HELL" or "Jahanna." These energy vortexes, which power their civilization, are located in these tunnels, along with precious stones and metals.

Battles have occurred both on Earth and in the skies. Arrangements and territories were established to maintain peace between the Dragonian devils and the Angels. For peace to be maintained, alliances were formed, and Dragonian Princesses were married off to seal these deals. One such princess gave birth to a son who was to rule Earth. Educated on Nibiru as a master scientist and builder, this son was part of the interplanetary federation's design, which initially did not include Earth.

Earth was originally a vacation spot or resort where beings from various galaxies and star constellations came to harvest minerals. This created clashes between the "ANGELGOONZ" and the enemies of "GOD" in Heaven, placing both sides in constant conflict due to the allure of evil and greed.

In Mother Africa, where everything on Earth began, the minerals are richer than anywhere else. This richness is a remnant of the paradise on Earth, the Garden of Eden, where laws were only those set by God. The classes and races established on Earth were initially set up in Africa, where melanin-rich people began life. Before Satan made evil appear fair-seeming, the Dragonian and serpent people created their own systems to maintain control.

To keep peace between Earth and these entities, marriages between the daughters of the Dragonian rulers and Earth's leaders were arranged. This practice mirrors how African tribes historically used marriage to maintain peace. Despite this, the interaction between the Annunaki and the reptilian side of Enki led to dominance by the reptilian aspect, which influenced behaviors such as a heightened focus on sexual activities with humans.

This dynamic is evident in the prevalence of sexual exploitation and the fascination with sex toys and beastiality, reflecting the ongoing influence of these ancient, deceptive forces.

However, they are still "abducting" humans for that purpose, and nobody is talking about it. As a matter of fact, Enki was significantly influenced by his reptilian side. He even allegedly went so far as to have intercourse with his daughters and granddaughter to "bear" a son who could assume key positions or compete with the sons of Nibiru.

In law, the rules of succession typically required that a son born to a male Annunaki and his half-sister would have succession rights. However, if the male Annunaki had a son by another woman who was not his half-sister, that son would not automatically have the same succession rights unless granted by the higher Annunaki. This rule made Enki extremely furious, as he believed that Enlil and his brother had stolen his birthright. He felt he should have been the ruler, not Enlil.

Well, well, well, Satan has some gangsters, but GOD has

some goonz—ANGELGOONZ—by Minister Melvin A. P.D.T.A.,

ANGELGOONZ

But having sex with his half-sister, Ninkarsag, who is also known as the Great Mother Goddess of Anunna, the giver of life and most revered provider for her children (also known as Anu's seed), was a scheme by Enki. Ninkarsag was to bear him a son. However, Anu did not bear him a son, only a daughter.

Here's how it went: The cunning Enki, in front of Nintu (Ninhursag), mother of the land, filled the ditches with his semen, overflowing into the reeds. His ritualistic acts, including the apron, bear resemblance to African rituals. Interestingly, George Washington was noted to have appropriated and participated in these rituals. Enki declared, "No one walks in the marshlands," and swore by the life of Anu that his semen belonged to one lying in the marshlands.

Enki directed his semen to dangle, and Ninkarsag, also known as Damakina, consented. Enki poured his semen into her womb. Over time, one day became a month, two days became two months, three days became three months, and so forth, until nine days, marking her ninth month. This cycle continued, culminating in the birth of

Naomi, who was three-quarters Annunaki and one-quarter Draco. Enki was furious because he wanted a son, not a daughter.

Yet Enki's schemes did not stop there. Naomi emerged from the bank of the river, and Enki, reaching out to his companion, Mud, asked, "Should I kiss the young one, the beauty?" His companion replied, "Kiss the young one, the beauty, for this will blow up the vigorous wind." This ability to control the weather is now mimicked by mankind, although the truth is still hidden.

Enki set foot in the boat, lodged it on land, and took Naomi. He kissed her and poured his semen into her womb. The same cycle followed: one day being one month, two days being two months, and so on, until nine months of womanhood. Ninkara was born, two-thirds Annunaki and one-third Draco. Again, Enki was left with a daughter instead of a son.

When Ninkara emerged from the riverbank, Enki asked Mud again if he should kiss the young one, the beauty. Mud's response was the same, and Enki followed through. This repetitive cycle is profoundly interesting and unusual, shedding light on our origins and current state.

But we must remember the evil to ensure we say "Never Again" and work together to grow. Good works go hand-in-hand with good. The most dreadful evil of all is turning kings and queens into "things." Satan has some gangsters hell-bent on white supremacy and division, but GOD in Heaven has some goonz— ANGELGOONZ—

by Minister Melvin A. P.D.T.A.,

As we continue to process all that is unfolding, it is important to note that "Abu" was a Mesopotamian god. When examining and piecing together these narratives, we confront deep questions and pains. For instance, the question is asked: "What hurts you?" The answer given is, "My legs hurt." This reflects the personal misery and burdens carried, symbolizing the weight of sins and the suffering experienced.

The ancient story goes that this anguish stems from a series of divine and earthly conflicts. Enki, once a powerful figure, was eventually confined to Nibiru and restricted from participating in its affairs. Ishtar, the goddess of love and fertility, played a significant role in these events. She attempted to free Enki, who had been imprisoned due to his tumultuous actions.

The narrative describes Dumuzi's relationship with Ishtar and how it demonstrated her dualistic nature as a liminal deity. Dumuzi's actions, including an alleged rape of his sister, led to his capture and eventual escape multiple times, which ultimately resulted in his death. This death was mistakenly attributed to Marduk, the god of Babylon, who had allegedly cloned an army to mimic himself. This practice of cloning is suggested to have been ongoing but hidden from the public.

Inanna accused Marduk of Dumuzi's murder, leading to a trial before the council of 24. Marduk was found innocent of the charges but was subject to complex divine judgments. The great deity faced resistance, which led to further turmoil and his eventual demise.

Marduk's case highlights the intricate divine laws governing succession and familial responsibilities. The law stated that if a brother died, his brother or father would take over the family and its responsibilities, including marriages and maintaining genetic purity. Inanna, seeking Nergal, a wise alchemist, faced opposition from Ereshkigal, the goddess of the underworld.

Inanna, who later became known as Ishtar, unknowingly conceived a child from her relationship with Dumuzi. This birth brought great distress as it was in violation of Annunaki laws, particularly regarding privacy. Nevertheless, Inanna gave birth to a son, Nanaya, described as being seven feet tall with black almond eyes and rich, melanin-rich skin. His voice was like the deep rushing waters of the ocean, symbolizing the black origin of all life.

This narrative illustrates the deep connections between divine actions and their impacts on human history and society. From kings and queens to the modern-day world, these stories remind us of the ongoing struggle between divine forces and earthly realities. In contemporary times, the fight against systemic injustice and division continues. As stated, "Satan's got some gangsters, and GOD's got some goonz—from 'A' to 'Z'—ANGELGOONZ"

by Minister Melvin A. P.D.T.A.,

Going deeper and deeper and getting deeper into "ANGEL-GOONZ," we learn of the evil of white supremacy but also that the real "Enemy" is The "Black" Man" To "Himself." Oh yeah, white supremacy exists, sure, and you better not get caught in the wrong place at all. But that goes for White People too, just not as much. But "Lynchings" do still occur, along with hangings of Black people. Still, you will never find a white person lynched and hanging from a tree behind or in front of Walmart. But "Blacks" yes, and they hide it.

See, God in heaven is raising and has raised up His "SUPREME ANGEL-GOONZ" to assist His holy Angels from Heaven to assist His Chosen "Present." Their "Avatar" absent, their spiritual actual bodies on the

"Mothership" as they rest and are awaiting their consciousness and spirit to return home to the Heavenly Father. But meanwhile, Satan's working, and "Dr. Claud Anderson" is a supreme "Angel-Goon" working hard on the front lines every day. Dr. Queen Vicki Dillard is a supreme "Angel-Goon." When the men don't step up, she steps up. And QUEEN, all the time, I love her.

"The Honorable" Elijah Muhammad" is a chief elder, the one prophesied about to come and awaken his people here in America. Like it or leave it alone, concerning whether or not if he was right concerning the teachings from "GOD" in person, "Master" FARD Muhammad. The grafting process of the white race to create evil on the earth is prophesied in the Bible of the original man being taken away. Even our cousins, who had been left in Africa where all life began, had been left and conquered the seas and came here to these Americas millions of years ago. We must not forget they had help from the evil side of the ANNUNAKI, whether or not you want to believe it or not.

Was damn near everything he said correct? Yes, everything concerning the evil and the Mothership, which they are now coming out admitting UFOs exist, and Jacob in the Bible assisted as "Yacub." Is his name, the letter J wasn't invented until about 500 years ago. Many question this, but God in the Bible says, "I Know What

You Know Not," concerning the evil of the new race. Jacob, Yacub, is allowed to bring into and onto the earth with the "shedding of the blood" of the "Original aborigines" of Africa and America. As we continue, Jacobite people came from "Nibiru" for the "gold." "Enki," Genesis before the flood, he was called "Mercury," and the devil is an attorney, and the doctor is too. Think about that. They're only here to help us live 60 years, only 60 minimum, but they want this world so bad that before they see any Black race return to "glory," they would rather blow it up or give it to foreigners. Nothing against foreigners; I love all people who love me, but let's get real. As we go deeper, they are even killing federal Black judges and Black U.S. government people who they feel get out of line every now and again, and people turn the other cheek. But we're dealing with receptor blockers related to the aging process.

The Lazarus group, Henry Kissinger, the Rockefellers, etc., are hiding age-reversing technology, chromosome stealth, sheath, telomeres. As you get older because of that. In the scriptures, God says our years are 120 years, and that His spirit will not always "strive" with man. They "stole our eternal life" by stealing and chopping off the "telomeres" in order for that to work. They use human growth hormones, and most of the food they give us to eat is banned in other countries. They are attacking us from every angle. Human growth hormone is what bodybuilders use, especially them. It's imperative to note that "Yacub's" grafted devils are not the White Race; only they are bound to be mixed in with us. Many ask how they were able to stop us from living so long. They went into the lab, of course. Now we understand they wanted us to live a short time, from 120 years to 60. In the "Sumerian" tablets, they talk about creating viruses to eliminate us all the time. And, believe it or not, they always call it "The Virus," an agent. And viruses do what? Spread.

Don't look to the government. Allegedly, "every" politician is an attorney, and all attorneys, that's what it says. But he who has ears to hear what the spirit has to say, let him hear it. And he who has eyes to see what the spirit has to reveal, let him see what the spirits have to reveal. Attorneys are good liars, my mama always taught me. And my mama is GOD too. It's imperative to note too that anytime we see "ELS," "EL," El Shaddai," "Enki," telling us it is all part of a special "GENETIC" program. So "cultivate" the land. Tend to the "cattle." And our bodies are made of what? Water too, with dirt, right? The land!

ANGELGOONZ By MINISTER MELVIN A.P.D. T.A.

All the minerals of the earth "Man" is indeed tied to, keeping that in mind, tied to the "Earth." And from the earth, we have 3 major "Cultures": 1) Tribes, 2) Families, 3) Clans. Everywhere Satan goes, he sows dissension. He comes, watches them fight, "The innocent" people of the earth, helps them start the war to begin with, then comes in and offers a solution "For a fee." Yacub left instructions for his "Grafted Devil" races: marry the lighter to the lighter always in order to continue until they got the race you see today with the help of the Annunaki. The others were made to blend in for "blending" purposes, all the way down until you get the recessive "blue" eyes and "blonde" hair race you see today. Groups of Europeans: "Nordic" tall warriors with long alkaline features and "Canaanites," short stubby curly hair Europeans that men also see today, they are called the Irish. So, you also got the white redhead boy with the woolly hair, Afro-Irish redhead child of Europe. But they tell us they don't like the Scottish to get to the Irish. But they tell us it's all about war: "Catholicism," original Irish derivative of "OREASHA." In fact, the Greeks were the first "civilization" "ANU" ordered to be cleaned up. She woke up and summoned the "Book Keeper," told him to "dispatch" the scientists to a place called the Caucasus Mountains. They came to find out they were living in caves with K-9s and on all fours. A throwaway genetic experiment. And where do we find all this? The

Sumerian Tablets using sulfur, which caused birth defects. "Carbon" and the ones that did not pass the test of standards were to be burned at "Gehenna," but sent in soul cycles, and they kept coming back "defective." And they couldn't get out of the earth's atmosphere; it's an energy flux. In 30 terms, denied the "RIGHT" to ascend. Now when they went and returned to the "Egyptian" hieroglyphics, it was said that "ISIS" brought a creature and said they were "From EUROPE." To her, they answered, and she said, "What type of creature is this?" She went on and asked, "What manner of beast is this?" They said, "Yacub's Grafted Devil." We must "remember," it is a war between two warring Annunaki family members, siblings' rivalry: one trying to stop the other. Enlil heard about the good times Enki was having on Earth with the "Earth" people and got jealous. The Bible says he is a jealous "GOD." It says, "I am a jealous God and thou shalt worship none but Me. Put no other God before Me," etc. But many say if he was a real God, and he is, that he wouldn't be worried about all that mess and "ish," as if he was the only God. Well, Satan's got some gangsters, God in Heaven's got some goons.

ANGELGOONZ BY MINISTER A.P.D.T.A.

ANGELGOONZ

Before I continue, I just want to thank you so much for making it this far, going deeper and deeper, connecting all the "dots." As it is written, "He who has ears to hear what the spirits have to say, let him hear what the spirits have to reveal." As we continue, it bothers me that my own race is not paying attention to all that's truly been going on: "Agenda 21," the truth, hate of self, and we are experiencing by overlooking all the "original truth" with fear-mongering through "white supremacy." This "beast" is going to always let us know He/She. Babylon, Babylon is "present" and ever ready to "exemplify" that Annunaki power from the evil side of the fallen angels with Annunaki experiments until they blended in with the albinos. The so-called Negroes, Oreos, are complicit heavily; they have been since the very beginning, helping and assisting "the evilness of white supremacy." Meanwhile, we must not forget that good exists in many of them because, after all, they do come from us through grafting. But the genetically malfunctioning laboratory of the imitators is here to create chaos. They are the rejects made by the evil side of the Annunaki, all because of jealousy between two siblings. They want us to believe that we can't function without all the wickedness, giving us "gods" and religions as controlling mechanisms and killing us all who not only "resemble" the Black African, the oldest man known, the first born of gods, first creation, proven all facts: all life began in Africa. And the Black African man is scientifically proven. But not only do they desire to eliminate through modern-day slavery, privatization, prison slavery, human system, allegedly collecting all the melanin, human waste, and doing something with it, but also they aim to eliminate the good white people who love Black people as well. And it's sad because while they got us fighting each other, the whole time, "all they wanted truly was one drop of our blood, and they would be able to ascend with us, the true aboriginals." They can't stop Black and white from loving each other. We will continue to fight to be free. We all have to live here. Get "over" it. Many of us love each other and have white in our family, and love exists here. Next, the money is next to control, and they're all over it. We didn't agree to any of this wicked-ness, but the evilness of the evil side of the Annunaki, who aided and continue to aid white supremacy, reptil-ians, sea people, and all its weird shit going on, please excuse my language. Lord God in Heaven, "Help" us. That's why we have earthly Angelgoonz. And the evil-ness is depending on us consenting to "false benefits," false treaties as always. They always make promises they never intend to keep, ever. And depopulation and more control over the people. Not just money, but every "resource": medical, education, the economic fields, etc. How much we make, how they tax us, etc. They always know this evil because they always replace one of their many evils with another evil. Remember when they said "no to drugs"? And then that TV dog taking a bite out of crime, then Smokey the Bear—a deeper conspiracy with the truth of evil setting fires on purpose, allegedly. Satan's got some gangsters. God's got some goons. ANGELGOONZ/107

"ANGELGOON" OH YEAH, WE HAVE WHITE "ANGELGOONZ," custodians of the Earth—so many I'll get into later on. But for now, back to business, FELLOW ANGELGOONZ. It is interesting; one may ask how we clean up the genetic defect—the defect of the human defect that was deliberately formed by someone playing "GOD" in the "laboratory" with "Jacob" (Yacub) simultaneously mixed in to blend in with human albinos and the "Annunaki" because of jealousy. What's the treatment? What's the remedy? Because they are going to keep coming back. If they try to use too much brain power, they will "shrivel up." That's why they invented "Artificial Intelligence" to think for them. The remedy is one drop of Annunaki blood and one drop of aboriginal blood from the people they claim to hate—the Black "race." The blood type tells them from whence they came. The blood types are "altered." The frequency of the "Earth"—well, Satan's got some gangsters; GOD HAS SOME GOONZ. ANGELGOONZ

by MINISTER MELVIN A. P.D.T.A.

· · ·

ANGELGOONZ

Ai is a strong force from the ANNUNAKI And, this technology has always been here as we al think its new Remember

Meopel, that's interesting. However, I see that American [something] are being [something] over one again. The sophistication of the Annunaki wants GOLD faster. They brought a "robot"—remember that can do everything as they desire to "replace us all with AI. It doesn't mean run from AI. All of this is going to trickle down to "COPS" being run by AI. NOW THAT'S SCARY BECAUSE OF "WHITE SUPREMACY" giving technology more and more power over us ALL. China has already started their conversion and is soon to be the TOP world power. Babylon, Babylon—the once great mother "WHORE"—successful because of her slavery and assistance from the "Annunaki" due to their deep hatred of the "Creator" and desire to "create" a dominant "race." Meanwhile, everyone is going to "EV" (Electric Vehicles). They always make the things they aim and desire to most "ENFORCE." They want to enforce more nano-technology. Now it's like we're being run through the "ringer." We don't know these people at all, but all we need to know is that Satan has some gangsters; GOD

HAS SOME GOONZ. ANGELGOONZ to fight in GOD's name—the real God, not wanna-bees or dilly-dilly-doo-dolly-go-along-to-get-along gods imitating the Most High through "tricknology." We aim to enjoy "peace," not war. But that's why they took the Black man out of the home originally—to start an eternal and internal war inside the original Black Native Americans. An "internal" war is "worse" than any war. Then they mixed all that up with the same people who claim they want to help Blacks, gave and implemented drugs, and every foul evil agency they could muster and think of to facilitate our downfall. They created these conditions to stop the Honorable Elijah Muhammad, Malcolm X, and the most Honorable Minister Louis Farrakhan from awakening us. A Chief Elder AngelGOON from GOD Almighty, Professor Smalls, is a Chief Angel Goon. We have many, thank GOD. And now they have pills for everything, and they tell us these pills are going to kill you. This way they cannot be held responsible; they think because they tell you these medications are going to kill you, according to "Galactic Law" and all the UFO stuff they have been hiding till now, everything is coming to a head, so to speak. As far as a vaccine is concerned, we never got any warnings, but now people are feeling the exact effects of taking the jab. Meanwhile, they're getting richer and richer off our suffering as a Black and white society who truly want to coexist in peace. Meanwhile, we are so uneducated, and that's the problem. Another thing is setting each other up to fail within our community is a taught behavior. Forcing drugs on our community didn't make it any better. Scamming each other is not the way to come up. Pooling all our resources together is a positive way to come up, but the Willie Lynch letters stopped that by promoting self "hate." The devil always uses our own people to infiltrate our own people's organizations and then take them over. They aim to get rid of the middle class altogether, and nobody's paying attention. However you chop it up, "ownership" needs to be at the forefront. Without ownership, you have no control. Putting everything in our "business" name—because as long as we are "citizens" they call us, even though we are the originals. As long as we are "visitors," the way they paint the picture telling "their" "vision" for us to believe, they control us and everything under Satan. Had us fighting in the 20s, 30s, 40s, 50s, and 60s for citizenship. Meanwhile, we didn't come over here in their damn ships. We don't need to be under their control; we are indigenous to these Americas. We outnumber them, so they're bringing in foreigners to further get rid of us, the original Black Indians, to keep from giving us what's "rightfully" ours. And if there is any type of era

. . .

Christian God, why aren't they exemplifying "Christ-like" behavior? All the roads lead to Rome, and they are forcing evil on us and taking our land and names. Religion and original spirituality are wrongfully twisted into paganism to steal, kill, and destroy in the name of Roman Christianity. Their numbers are declining so badly that they are now calling on all the groups that helped them take us and everything we ever stood for, including GOD in Heaven. Now, they are begging everyone they killed, the so-called Jews spoken of by Jesus in the Bible—an intelligent people with many who have helped us a lot of times, though with "strings attached." Nevertheless, there are good Jewish people who love Blacks and know the real truth. But they need their numbers to go up, and every group they've wronged for foreign soil is now being called upon to help them steal from us—the real Aborigines of these Americas. So everyone takes a piece of our pie except us, all in the name of their Jesus.

The majority of the foreigners they let come over here don't have hair of wool or skin of bronze; many are melanin-deficient. Now, they need everyone they made a generational pact with to help each other keep the Blacks down by turning the other cheek. And Black people do it to each other every day—turn the other cheek, a "blind" eye. Many are originally from the Annunaki, and white supremacy blinds them. Before all the "chickens" come home to roost, "White Supremacy" wants a fighting chance, so they need their numbers to go up to compete with what's coming to them for their evil against Blacks. That's why they rely so heavily on Artificial Intelligence as well.

But God has taught me that every ally they believe is going to have "their" backs will, in fact, turn on them. Because of their past as a great nation, as a result of the Blacks, for personal greed, selling their souls to Satan to gain the whole world, and purposely stealing everything from the Aborigines of this land they claim they discovered, America knows this to be true. She's a devil, and devils know devils, but she would rather die and kill everybody before she returns what is rightfully ours or even treats us fairly at all. Please know that life is cyclical; if you interpret the patterns, your "breaks" in the "cycles upon cycles," the trick is to learn the "lessons" to allow us to see when the cycles flip so we can jump out of the infinity loop when it comes around, so we won't get caught in it because it's coming to America no matter how safe she thinks she is. So we can jump out of it. The Law of the Gods, Galactic Federation Law, states that when you do something in a free-will universe to deprive the original people and all people of good through free will, you will be subjected to the same punishment. America knows this, which is why she's scared.

Now we always hear, "What goes around comes around," "Reap what you sow," "You get out what you put in," "Do unto others as you would have them do unto you," but America does the opposite. She does evil over good every time because of her hatred for GOD in Heaven. Everything GOD in Heaven says not to do, America says to do. Galactic Law has us in this position because of dirty conditions. The "Queen of Heaven and Earth" wants to clean up this big, big mess of white Annunaki mess. We are helping GOD in Heaven, His elite Angelgoonz, from large and minute. We are here—like it or let it alone. Oh yes, Galactic Law has us truly in this because of a dirty "prior" condition, with all the Angelgoonz from Dr. King, the Honorable Elijah Muhammad, the Honorable Minister Louis Farrakhan, and President Lyndon B. Johnson is a

ANGELGOONZ

Tied to the Earth, we traverse to different locations. Ultimately, it is the frequency of the Earth that is changing. This begins with the Annunaki assertion and invention of their "blond hair, blue eyes" which is different from the white race invented by Jacob/Yacub. It's important to remember that the letter "J" wasn't invented until about 500 years ago. The blending of these two races and the promotion of white supremacy through groups like the

KKK only serves to create division, keeping the Aboriginal Black Indigenous people asleep and in a stupor.

The efforts of Lyndon B. Johnson, an "Angelgoon," were made to do right in a world of white supremacy. In a world where illusions of glitter and play are presented, the traps set against Blacks were under Rome's guidance, with England and Portugal also being complicit in these evils. President Johnson may not be a saint to everyone, but he did what God compelled him to do in the realm of civil rights.

As we move forward, Angelgoons must understand that our frequencies are deep because we are organic to the land. We are tied to the Earth like a radio, which needs to be properly tuned to stay in tune. To keep us from turning into a genetic "mush," we must remain compatible with the Earth. So why not remain here in peace? God is weeding out all the imitators; otherwise, the Earth would pull us apart in a world filled with so much hate. They call it gravity, but God has taught me that it is actually an electromagnetic field that plays a crucial role in this process. This energy creates the illusion of gravity, which, by the way, is the weak force. The magnetic field maintains its position according to the rays and waves of the electromagnetic field.

Geneticists are working to enforce Yacub's rule. We know Yacub is a Black Jew. Why is this important? The

Holy Bible talks about impostor Jews. Was Jacob an impostor Jew? Or was Yacub the real Jew?

The Jews come from Jacob, the Judeans. The Black Judeans are the children of Jacob. Jacob is Yacub, the supplanter who comes to replace the original man. It is imperative to note that The Honorable Elijah Muhammad said when Yacub started enforcing his rule, they were using the police. There were no police here before they came with their serpents from Angola—the spoils of war. We were among those they warred with, and spoils include women, children, oil, gold, etc. Now we are warring mentally, seeking documents to guide us. They made this oath publicly, and someone has to expose it.

Now let me ask you: What do they call it when you have one drop of so-called Negro blood in America? The answer is "Negro." How much Annunaki blood will it take to clean up the genetic mutation? Just one drop. And that's not a coincidence.

Now that we have that out of the way, my fellow Angel-goons, why do they call America the "Great Melting Pot"? What do you do in a melting pot? You mix ingredients together. Eugenicists, who are known for their experiments, studied the uncanny attractions of Blacks and were astonished by the beauty of Black women. They were amazed and compelled to study further. They couldn't figure out why the white woman didn't find the Black man appealing. How are they going to get a drop of blood if they don't understand these dynamics?

To attract and draw together two opposing forces, you need to reverse the resistor, which inverts the current of one force, causing them to draw together. In essence, creating attraction between opposites involves altering the dynamic to ensure they are drawn to each other.

Now, beloved reader, let me ask you: What does everyone want? They want what they can't have. So, how do you enforce getting the opposites to attract to each other? While we are advised to stay away from "White Sally" and "Karen," George Wallace, who left office in 1979 but re-entered politics and won his final term as governor in 1982, stood with the KKK and was adamant about protecting the so-called purity of the white race, particularly the white woman, at all costs. But how could he do that?

We understand the dynamics of the KKK and their role in perpetuating white supremacy. Many refuse to acknowledge this and resist being under anything as hateful as white supremacy, which is directed against Blacks. However, many whites may be surprised to discover they have Black ancestry, though it is alleged.

Historically, they originally came from Barcelona, Spain, where the Black hand, the grand dragon, led the coneheads across the land.

Before using pale faces to infiltrate Black institutions and keep us out, they held secrets in hidden lodges, such as the 32nd-degree Scottish Rite Masonic lodge. They employed reverse psychology to draw the two groups together, though most still fail to understand this. They drew the two together by telling them they couldn't have each other. We're dealing with long-term thinkers, far removed from the cave days.

In Genesis, they describe efforts to eliminate the birth defect in Europeans. Ironically, Dr. Frances Cress Welsing identified this defect, which stopped many from achieving ascension. God, Big Mama (Mother Nature), and BGI do not approve of this, as she says you can't throw people away.

We thought we were on the brink of being last, but we were living as the last because we are the first. We live as the last to those who were last of the first that God in Heaven made, not the Annunaki. Since Satan has some gangsters, God also has some goons—Angelgoons.

As stated by Minister Melvin A. P.D.T.A.,

.   .   .

ANGELGOONZ

The Devil's 6,000-year rule is the fact that "Evil" made fair "seeming" of Enlil's plan. Satan's plan is to "Turn" our Earth into "our" own hell by not allowing us to "Experience" our own "Heaven" on Earth. The plan is simple: for the "Darker" people, especially the so-called Blacks and the poor, to continue to create a heaven on Earth for Satan to rule. Enlil's Annunaki plan of white supremacy spreads war everywhere, kills, steals, and destroys, and treats the poor like a toy. Because they did their dirt, the good had to and has to suffer with the bad. When you get so comfortable living a high-society life-style to please an evil god, it is insane considering the soul and this body as an "Avatar". They continue to make Satan shine brighter as if he is the creator. In reality, Satan is only the creator of an excellent illusion and continues to do wicked and resist God in Heaven and our struggle.

But in order to win against white supremacy, we first have to wake up from our slumber and brainwashing and stop playing stupid. There are good white people who love Black people and the poor, and those are who we are to be friends with—friends from Da F to The Z. We must recognize that the devil is in place to use the "LAW" because it wasn't here before they came over. We didn't have prisons; we got outsmarted. They were doing blood rituals we didn't know how to break from under the curse. Remember again, they want us to stay away from Vodou, but they were doing blood rituals.

They believe in real Christianity, which is fair only in evil made to appear fair seeming. Since we didn't know how to break away from under their evil curse, it only made us incapable of learning because it kept our brain in a stupid spell of deep, deep sleep. And because the Angels can't function in a state of fear, the fear causes all of our auras to shrink like a deflated ball, creating our own hell and making us bow down to something inferior.

As we know, historical records are being put together, and genetic practices are being spoken of in ancient times. The scrolls and all the storytelling say the same thing indirectly and directly: you're not being punished for your sins; you're being punished by your sins. So who are they using to "thrash" us across our backs? That too has a lifespan and comes to an end. AI and technology are so sophisticated that for them to continue this evil is madness—but it can't continue on, PERIOD. The so-called Blacks are tired, and so are all the genuine people, white, etc., who love Blacks. We ask: are there any more melting pots?

The Brazilianization of mixing up a genetic pool to clean the birth defects from an inferior stock by the royal blood from across the land. The American priest was led and infatuated and most effective in recovering Yacub's grafted devil. Who did they really say The Honorable Elijah Muhammad said would get rid of them? He said reverse engineering them. So if they get one drop of the blood of the original man, woman, and child, that's enough to allow them to ascend to heaven because now they can raise the sacred secretion for a particular function. Before, they could only operate on the silver liquid, which is what they call the cerebrospinal fluid, which is clear like water and heavily infused with colloidal gold and silver metals. YES, METALS. "ARE Y'ALL ALRIGHT?" Essential metals. It's not until the soft metals come into the body—what we call "toxic" metals—that interfere with inflammatory harmony in the system, allowing the secretions to rise. That's why they also put it all in our water, food, air, etc. As we continue, ANGELGOONZ, Satan's got some gangsters; GOD'S GOT SOME GOONS.

ANGELGOONZ BY MINISTER MELVIN A.P.D.T.A.

ANGEEGOONZ

They have, whenever it is said "soul," because of the "Decasification" of that channel which allows the "Secretion" to arise in the pineal gland. They couldn't raise the liquid from the base of that race or races from the spine to the head. It causes them to short circuit and makes them "Operate and function on a very 'LOW' vibrational level," thinking below the waist always, and on lower "Chakras." They can't get past that. All they really needed or need is one drop of "Original" blood to "Clear" the "Channel." Eugenicists were out telling the public they were trying to "Keep" us all apart—Black and white —but were actually behind the scenes "Promoting Inter-racial Relationships" because they knew the "Pure" truth. To clean up the "Genetic" Defect, the quality of or the condition of the original "Man" of the planet is where you get and find all the answers. That's why they constantly experiment on nobody else on the planet except the Black man, woman, and child. Mainly us, because we have a direct bloodline connection with God in Heaven, and the only thing the enemy can do is "Play" God, "Play" us. But they can never be us, so they imitate and annihilate.

See the quality or control conditions having "Strong" Reproductive Powers—generation with full "Fertility" between different species or races, specifically between "Hybrids" of the 1st generation. Allowing people who didn't have the right to ascend would then now have the right to ascend. So now it all makes sense, "Perfect" sense. Why we tolerated all the hell they inflicted on us, all the pain they continue to inflict, as we could have risen up at any moment and rebelled tremendously and taken over under our oppression and didn't even know it. Freedom was the chicken on the stick, and so-called niggers love chicken, they say. And they had the stick tied behind our backs. So when we were chasing chicken —which is the most poisonous outside of pork, which Jesus put the demons in as He healed and cured people —He couldn't find any other animal dirty enough to put demons and nastiness in because a pig doesn't "sweat," so it keeps all the sin and filth and evil inside.

But speaking of chicken, we were chasing the chicken, and we were the ones distributing "Freedom" across the land. All we have to do is remember who we "ARE" and give the order to restore the "Balance" to the land, the water, and the Galactic Law. Anything or any organization "Functional" enough to "Aid" on the planet to assist must mobilize. But as The Most Honorable Elijah Muhammad, Malcolm, The Most Honorable Minister Louis Farrakhan, President Johnson, and all God's ANGELGOONZ BLACK tried and must continue to try on the planet and jointly mobilize to truly clean it up. And yes, God has white ANGELGOONZ who worked behind the scenes and did and do what they could, but it's deeper because the evil is so far-seeming.

But to clean all that up is to clean up the water, air, and sea. What used to be chemtrails is cleanup stuff now, but it too has to come out of the sky and bring all the foul stuff that mankind made with it in order to get it all out of the air. God's ISIS has to send the flood, washing it all off the land. Let he who has not sinned cast the first "Stone," so it can then travel, flowing into underground chambers of filters—charcoal, which by the way, is better than "Baking Soda." But anyway, the soils of the Earth. So now whenever we continue to see flooding in dry places, we should all know why. Now remember, they still have flooding in California, Mexico, etc. Pay attention because it's a desert. Maybe we should go visit the Orisha/Orishapatriarch who brings drought. Scarring with scars in the process of drought when, after all, the "Matriarchal" comes. The payout comes in the "Transferring" of the energy "From" Aquarius. ANGEL-GOONZ, well, Satan's got some gangsters; God in Heaven has some GOONZ from A to Z—ANGELGOONZ.

By MINISTER MELVIN A.P.D.T.A.

ANGEEGOONZ

Continuing On As we go deeper into ANGELGOONZ, pieces of which are connected to Aquarius—which is the water from pieces to Aquarius, which is ultimately the "air"—moisture evaporation, the reverse of "evaporation," is called "Saturation." So, the water "Picture" of Aquarius in order to signal the return of the "Aquarian

Age" is all signals in "Stars" flying through that way. That, in fact, deliberately "Way Aquarius Clears" AHHHHH the return of the sweet water "Washing" away all the evil toxins on the Earth "ISIS" through and out the "BOWELS" of the planet to be cleaned because it's imperative that we clear the land and clean the land. But we first have to no doubt start with the air. Through the evaporation, we transfer the process in which it was placed where it didn't ordinarily "Rain" in order for such to happen in the upper "Atmosphere" because we do indeed have those atmosphere "Rivers," which have to change trajectory under given forces in order to switch where the condensation of the Earth arises.

Because the UV rays of the sunlight connect with the people of the royal family—the "NOBLE" blood—because of the Earth-born "stardust" accumulation to the unique physical body. Earth-born child of the "Stars" Explanation. You have to be on and vibrate on a certain high spiritual vibrational frequency in order to be optimally and functionally here, and if you have someone here denied the right to be "Optimally" functional, well, in that situation, Satan's got some gangsters; God's got some Goonz—ANGELGOONZ.

Yahweh is Enki. They gave birth to a virtuous she who was 5/8 Annunaki and told to stay in the house and have nothing to do with Enki unless he brought her some delicacies. Filling the ditches with water, he filled the canals, even on unsown land. In his joy, the gardener hugged him and said to him, "Who are you? Who has watered my garden?" Then Enki answered Anu, "Bring me the delicacies." Then they brought them—all of the delicacies—and helped them up. Enki's face turned green, so he grabbed the staff and headed out to make demands in her house. "Anu, open up. You're at my door. Who are you?" He answered, "Anu, I am the gardener who will give you the delicacies as a reward."

But it was asked before, "Who is this 'Pale' Faced Creature lacking Melanin? What is the manner of this? The nature of this?" They, however, continued on, recognizing the true real nature of things as it is all coming out now. Her heart left as he, Anu, opened the door of the house. Enki, to the virtuous woman, gave the delicacies. The woman clapped her hands at the goodness of originality and dismissed her earlier attention away from evil. Enki became aroused, took her, lay in her lap, stroked and massaged her body. He pierced her, kissed her. Enki poured the semen into the womb; she drew the semen into the woman. Enki's semen, due to the seductive woman, said aloud the power in the body: "Oh, this is power inside my body! Oh, the power!" Even outside, made upset and angry, Ninkharsag wiped the semen from his body. Ninkharsag, daughter of Anu.

So in some way, evil put eight plants to poison Enki. They took specimens from a laboratory and, through "Genetic Manipulation," identified identical mutations similar to "Yacub" and so on. As white power uses Blacks as guinea pigs and abuses the bodies of the original man in hopes of making their bodies better, melanin is needed at a very high level. After all this, they are still at it today. However, these created eight daughters called plants for reproduction. Their names are Baima, Nintula, Ninsutu, Ninkasi, Sisiana, Azimn, and they are all trained in the arts of lost morals. That's right, beloved, lost morals—sex, lingam, or snake charming. But the quickest way a woman can control a man was their expertise. They were the most beautiful of maidens, their job being solely to seduce Enki. Their plans, with Enki and his womanizing, fell hard, immediately into so much as to throwing out all his...

Mates and then reconstructing his whole damn household around her private monkey—her "Pleasure," that is. Around these eight most luscious sex deities, the hurry more in his old age. The soul of Enki fell seductively and passionately out of control, controlling him with that monkey between her legs. He began to drink, gluttoning and self-overindulging until his countenance fell beyond the degree of deity. He was poisoned, sick, and ready to die. It was ordered, Ninkharsag was ordered to take away the curse. She ordered the hurry to abandon him, whereupon she took a unique interest in his health and did nurse him back to health.

Ninkharsag fixed Enki in her certain fungi genitalia, including the labia majora, labia minora, and her clitoris. She had sex with him—plain and simple; sex heals, as we see here. I could go off into other aspects here; however, you get the point. In some circumstances, brother, it is asked, "What hurts you?" He said, "My skull hurts me." "I have caused Naima to be born for you, brother."

"Brother, what hurts you?" "My jaw hurts me." "I have caused Mora to be born for you."

Again, it is asked, "Brother, what hurts you?" "My tooth hurts me." "I have caused Ninka Si to be born for you."

"Brother, what hurts you?" "My throat hurts, my mouth hurts because I have caused Susana to be born."

"Brother, what hurts you?" "My arm hurts me." "I have caused Asthma to be born for you."

"Brother, what hurts you?" "My ribs hurt me." "I have caused so much to be born for you."

Satan's got some gangsters; God's got some "GOONZ"— ANGELGOONZ.

By Minister Melvin A. P. D. T. A.

AngelGoonz

Oh, oh, "GOD" of all the planets, "LORD" of all the "WORLDS" and all the "UNIVERSE," "ANU" is our Father who art in "Heaven," who became "Earth" and "Tammuz." What is imperative to note is that "ISHTAR," "Dumuzid," or "Tammuz" are the protagonists in one of the world's first love stories. Courtship, however, "DUMUZID" or "TAMMUZ," the shepherds, and "Ningishzida" are the two doorkeepers of ANU. Tammuz is the child who became God on Earth. That's right, he finished his schooling amongst the issue of love. He was also known as Aponis, a leader of the Armanian Hebrews.

Inanna arrived at the underworld, called "Hell," with another intent to win the favor of the "Rich" people, which would no doubt be in the favor of the Irish in persuading the freeing of her grand uncle "ENKI," because beloved, she could always persuade "ENKI" to do her will. As long as he was confined to "Carnegie"/"HELL" by orders of Anu, she would not exercise her free will. So their plans also included freeing "ENKI" from his 10-year jail term for trying to deceive others by having a son by her diverse honor. He wanted another son for the purpose of succeeding him because his son "Marduk" would not do it. Being his grandfather,

Anu had gotten the scholarship in the school called Haka or "TAHUTI," who also became "Yaanuwn," one of the 24 elders, a being of truth. Marduk was the first disagreeable to attend there at the school, indeed disagreeable. But "Tehuti" is the self-created. When he finished the school, he was also known as "MICHAEL" or simply "MALACHI," and he became "The MELCHIZEDEK" of Aramance Hebrews.

Khidr is in Islam what "Elijah" represents in Islam. To the Jewish people, it is very important and imperative that we, as we all "Study" ANGELGOONZ, recognize that the original "Jews" were "African" before being robbed of the knowledge of self and infiltrated. Various Islamic and non-Islamic traditions recognize Khidr as an angel, prophet, wali who guards the "Sea" and teaches knowledge. This makes you wonder about all the sea humanoids and later on robotoids—anything to blend in. Al-Qada of the Syrians, Muhammad, and between the two is the Grecian Christians. These three schools are physical schools related to Hinduism, Hindu incarnations, or spiritual schools: Christianity, Judaism, and Islam—all come from Hinduism allegedly, and Confucianism and Buddhism. YES, BUDDHISM. Speaking of Buddhism, did y'all know Buddha was originally "BLACK"?

Anyways, they traveled from the Far East Asia across to the Middle Eastern Asiatic and now have invaded the Western world of white supremacy. As we go deeper, all of these six, numbered as 1) Hinduism, 2) Confucianism, 3) Buddhism, 4) Hebrewism, 5) Christianity, and 6) Muhammadism, are all responsible for thousands of the religious sects on Earth and denominations that control the minds of humans. The robotoids and sea people are simply trying to follow suit but trying to keep up maintenance to the best of their abilities as they are programmed. Everything we encounter as a people is always planned 10 to 20 years in advance, which is why they keep us programmed so we don't wake up and continue to break down as well. These are the roots of all planned evil against God, though intended for good by GOD, but "Mankind" corrupted them by making evil fair-seeming.

These are the six degrees of six, either in mystical order or sin, represented by the female deity called the Blessed Mother Mary, which is also called the Mother. The mysteries of Assad as Isis, her trinity name, when they use the name Mary, they never tell us the degrees of Mary. 1) The Hebrew Mary, sister of Moses. 2) The Greek Mary. 3) Mariam. 4) Mary Magdalene. 5) Mary, daughter of Joachim and Anna, supposedly the mother of Christ—not Mary but Mariam. The story of Joachim, his wife Anna (or-Anna), and the miraculous birth of

Jesus was told in the 2nd century apocryphal Infancy Gospel, the Gospel of James (also called the Protoevangelium of James). Joachim was a rich and pious man who regularly gave to the poor. Mariam, from the ancient Hebrew black origin, meaning their rebellion degree. Mariam the Hebrew, then you have the 2nd degree, the Greek Mariam, which the Bible calls Mary. Finally, Mary of the ANGELGOONZ—Mary the Muhammad, which all relates to the three meters of Masham, Messiah, and Muhammad, and Mariam, which is the Tamarind, the wife of Muhammad. Each had their Mary: Mariam, Moses' sister; Mary Magdalene, Jesus's wife; and Mary, Muhammad's last wife to seal the deal of ANGELGOONZ.

The evils of white supremacy indeed persist. Since Satan's got some gangsters, God in Heaven's got some GOONZ. Satan does, especially in America in politics, etc. They dominate the world of gangsterism; they glorify it and continue to oppress the poor, especially the original man, woman, and child who were already here and are indeed native to the Americas long before Columbus.

Well, since Satan's got some gangsters, God's got some GOONZ to help all His Aboriginals and His people— good people, no matter the color. But it just so happens that the most common color of people committing the most evil all over the world is linked to white supremacy. Satan's got some gangsters; God's got some GOONZ—ANGELGOONZ.

By MINISTER MELVIN A. P.D.T.A.,

ANGELGOONZ

To balance it all out and to make it all make sense, Almighty God in Heaven had to raise up and continues to raise up His "Angel Goonz." And they are not messing around. We know full well that Angel Goonz only follow one tune: the tune that vibrates on a very high vibrational frequency and are willing to die to see God's people free, regardless of what anyone may think. Please, as you read this, don't blink. Although, truthfully, overstand or if you're used to being controlled, understand that Angel Goonz are here.

One doesn't need to look too far or go too far. Just look at all the evil done to a people called Black people who helped save the oppressors from the Black Plague—a loving people, spiritual by nature, directly from Almighty God in Heaven. The Lord God says in Genesis, "Behold," telling us to look, and some other beings behold the "Man"—of course, Adam. The man has become one of us, classifying himself as one of us,

Hebrew, not Greek. Genesis 3:23 tells us that Jehovah takes on a physical form as Elohim, the mighty one. So God is judging over all the gods.

However, it is all tied to what we are seeing today. The enemy just programs the programmable, and evil follows suit. The so-called African Americans were just a way to steal our indigenous land and all we are—a people, the first people of God on Earth, made a mockery by a people in power who are afraid of all the evil they have done to us. They fear that if they give us any real chance, we will come up quick, awaken our people, and begin to live, I mean really "live."

For the love of their god Satan, they don't want us alive physically, mentally, or spiritually. They want us to not live but to "die," afraid of what they did to us we might do to them. But that is not true. This is the evil brought down by the Annunaki, the wicked side of white supremacy and greed. White gangsters in politics, on a very high political level, suppress the Blacks. It's crazy because the music executives own the prisons that the rappers rap about killing and dealing. We do love to see our youth rich and thriving, but not at the expense of losing Black lives. It's all about the "melaninated" body and organ harvesting. They hate us but love our precious Black body organs because our organs are good, but they use and do bad, evil things to steal them.

Low vibrational music is only to control the Blacks and lead them to prison, turning them into "punks" and taking over the alpha Black man. And who is left to take the Black "booty"? The key to long life? The Black woman? They replace the Black man with everyone else but himself by setting evil traps of entrapment. You would have to be a devil to do all of the above and keep their feet on our necks until the world ends. They think artificial intelligence is going to help them beat God in Heaven. But God says we are the first and we will be the last. We have no birth date or history, so the enemy is trying to create our death date as a so-called race. We, the Blacks, have been here since the very beginning, and we have all the answers. They know this, but as we soon shall see, moving right along, these are the "schools" of sisters in wonder, who will be holograms, self-proclaimed prophets, and types of evil tricknology.

Technology is what they are working on, called polarities—reversing the polarities in our brains. They use fluoride to calcify the pineal gland, the eye of the Black God. I say Black because we are Black, and according to the Bible, so is the one they call Jesus. The polarities in our brains are attacked to block all communication to Jesus, God, and everything needed to wake us up. That's why they invented and flooded our Black neighborhoods with it and every other trap.

. . .

Using a religion to follow and a Jesus who is depicted as white as a savior—this is all part of the evil that masquerades as good. Now, as we wake up, Melchizedek, who is Marduk, can best teach, train, and motivate us. Melchizedek himself has gone through transformation, dealing with false accusations and conflicts.

Ashtar had decided to go to the underworld with the intention of having a son by Nergal, the brother of Dumuzi. She was struck by a rich one with a laser gun and was left for dead. All those technologies we see in movies—where do you think they came from? Enki couldn't help her, and neither could her father. As time passed, Ishtar was slowly dying, and a risk eagle could not heal her.

So, the ruler Anu projected a hologram of himself and commanded a risk eagle to rescue Ishtar. She was taken to her mother Ningal to be nursed back to life. Once Ishtar was well again, she was summoned to the council of the great Annunaki. She repented of her wrongdoings and apologized for the conflicts she had caused. She promised not to deceive her family again and was granted forgiveness.

Ishtar was worshipped as a great deity, symbolizing both war and peace. She became the high priestess of the temple of Ishtar and was worshipped as the universal mother of all things. To this very day, Inanna (Ishtar) is still worshipped. Her symbol, the mother and child, represents Ishtar and Tammuz, also known as the Black Madonna.

No wonder so much has been hidden from us. It's too much for some to stomach. They say the rabbit hole goes very deep, but Angel Goonz don't eat rabbit. We possess the spirits of God in Heaven, fighting for good habits. Everything started with us, so-called Black people. As time passed, statues and pictures telling us who we really were were stolen. The real Black Madonna and child manifested here and everywhere across the world. In China, she is known as Aphrodite. In Israel, she is Ashtaroth. In Rome, she is Venus. In India, she is Devaki. And the list goes on.

No matter how much they try to steal, kill, and destroy, they can't escape our true, rich, God-given identity. They hide it because of their guilt, and they want to eat us alive as well. We must not focus on this, but rather on learning and creating a way out of white supremacy. This involves working with those of any other race who desire to see us truly free.

You want to know how good or evil a nation is? My God in Heaven says: "Give the nation power, and that nation will show you exactly who and what it truly is." Full of devils, there's nothing heavenly about it. The bombings of other nations, creating conflicts, and robbing Africa—originally our lands—of natural resources like oil, gold, platinum, and diamonds, are all parts of the hell they have made for us. Earth is a living hell for Black people during the Annunaki reign.

While people lived somewhat normal lives with laws and morals, Enlil saw evil as good. Satan's got some gangsters, but God's got some "Goonz." Angel Goonz,

by Minister Melvin A. P.D.T.A.,

ANGELGOONZ

We have white Angel Goonz with "black hearts" that love Blacks as I love whites. The brilliant and brave Jane Elliott is brave and bold for risking her life to teach the truth. She doesn't proclaim to be a lying self-proclaimed prophetess; she is noble in her own right. Professor Smalls, Dane Calloway, 19 Keyz, and Billy Carson are extreme Angel Goonz. With the exception of Ms. Elliott, these all come down from the goodness seed of the Annunaki. These beloved people all work hand in hand in their own rights and blessings and gifts of boldness.

But all Blacks coming into the knowledge of self are Angelic Goonz utilizing mathematics as a guide, working hand in hand with white Angel Goonz to truthfully awaken the masses of the original native people of this land with the truth in hope of truthfully being free. True freedom starts with the truth.

Now, many may not believe that white and everyone living comes from the Black man, but I don't see why not, seeing that the Black man is the first man on Earth. But moving right along, it is very imperative to note that Africans were here in these Americas for well over 400 to 10,000 years before Jesus. But moving along concerning the Annunaki, different than others, there were no limits—wives, children, etc. They lived as normal people; they were the spooks that sat by the door. Mysteries or what the Torah, the Bible, and the Quran portray as Angels were people whose image and likeness you, Black man and original woman, were procreated from.

I must admit, beloved, as we go deeper into Angel Goonz, these are three stages of the Annunaki: the 1st Anu, the 2nd Etherian, and the 3rd Risian, descended in density levels to become the Etherians. The Etherians incarnate as Riskians, either defused or risky, and are born on the planet Risk. Risk is broken up into three mysterious continents; allegedly some of the Annunaki reside on Kuzmista. The Romanians or "Greys" that nobody wants to talk about, who were also created by the Riskians, live on Parania because they did come before the Galactic Council of 24.

And all this is very, very, very important to overstand. Hollywood—Holly-weird—is putting it all right in front of our faces, and nobody's paying attention. And as far as inventing on Earth, it belongs to the Black man, as everything believed to be white inventions is, in fact, stolen from Blacks to push white superiority and dominance. The evil side of Enlil and its schemes make our children believe we never invented anything but crime, while they were the real criminals the whole time.

With the Greys, it was asked by them to provide protection from the reptilians to the council, due to the reptilians pursuing them like bounty hunters to enslave them and use them as guinea pigs. "Sound familiar"? This means they used genetics as whites use genetics on Blacks every day. Black people don't even know about it —splicing and cloning. Everything they can under white power and complete domination is about controlling slave people and slave food. They control the places of Blacks and the things back to the wickedness.

Would have to go to these reptilians to reproduce, so they did that and returned to the Riskians. They love to take risks. Once the planet was safe again to inhabit, they asked if they could be of service to stay there, and the Riskians agreed that they would be perfectly

Suited for reconstructing the atmosphere and domes because of all the high radiation that "surrounded" the planet when the shield was depleted. When the "job" was completed, they were given citizenship in "Risk" and even their own planet in Amaten. They were given a one "moon planet" truly not far from Risk that evolved around one of the three suns and sunshine. This planet was called Lydian. Others chose to live next to their creators on "The Planet Risk" on the continent Parunya or Darunya. Others being from other stars were referred to as the "visitors" of the three suns: Nowaubian, with three continents: 1. Zarantu, 2. Darnurniva, and 3. Kusmusta. Black Chosen Black Land and they are allowed to visit other continents. But as we talk about aliens, the other beings can visit with an "escort" and are not allowed to spend even one complete Riskian "day" there. We must overstand the Riskians who inherit the name and Annunaki. When they came, they were called Alum. They have three (3) stages: (1) Denier, (2) Ruins, which is the soul, and (3) The Etherians. Well, Satan's got some gangsters. God's got some GOONZ ANGEL-GOONZ FROM "A" TO "Z". ANGELGOONZ

BY MINISTER MELVIN A. P.D.T.A.,

. . .

ANGELGOONZ

Which is the spirit and, the "Riskians" called the Bashrins which is the body "beloved." They do not live on the "Planet Risk" they only hover around the planet "Risk" as "Fols" of the air "hovering" around, landing at "will" anytime they get ready. It's very imperative to "note" that the "Riskians" came in and out of the "Risk" atmosphere in which the "Ethereans" do "protect" with a "dome" they built for them all to live "under," which they live in the "atmosphere" of air. Those are the 3 "stages" of "Riskians": they are not seen but, they are felt. The "Ethereans" are seen only as light, and the "Annunaki" are seen "physically." It takes a "Riskian" of at least 9000 "years" to be "conceived." "Riskians" come down and you humans, we humans, come up. Meaning "humans" go from "babies" to adults to "old" age, which is fish greater to spirits being in three stages which gives you who are equals creatures force of will and equals the Tamarine deity of fertility depicted as an erected phallus, protector of fertility, sexuality, male genitalia, livestock, gardens, crops, fruits, and merchant sailors. While the "Riskians" go from this to the Ethereans, humans go from "radical" to student to discipline, and "Riskians" go from disciplined to student to "radical." Our death is their "life" and our life is our death, all by design, which is the type of evil in why white supremacy thinks they own the blacks all by design and, believe they can never allow us "blacks" to ever be truly free. So they draw off of everything they tell us "blacks" to stay away from, their "white" privilege, white dominance, they study it all, everything they don't want you to study including the supreme "mathematic" vudu, voodoo, hoodoo, etc. They use these powers against us every day. Where do you think they got them "from" in the 1st place? Jealousy because we are direct descendants of God with a direct bloodline to our creator. The truth hurts. You don't just move to a colder climate and lose melanin. Blacks have been moved around to climates different from time to time over slavery and all over the world, and we don't lose melanin unless they cause it. And, death is what you call heaven there, as far as they can discern on earth. They dance on these other planets, the "Riskians" and the "Etherians," as we do on earth. They watch holograms. However, they do not have pets as humans do and don't subject anything there in heaven. Their "ego" doesn't appear or depend on the subjugation of creatures like white supremacy does to blacks like animals. And, there is no divorce on "Risk" heaven because there is no marriage. The marriage of "Dumuzy" and Inanna was performed in the temple of "Harappa" on earth when the "Annunaki" lived amongst or are they still here????? The "beings" on earth performed peace sake incorporated their "culture," which is included. Marriage rituals and many other things strange to them. There are disagreements, there are rules, of course, that govern truth, and those rules are dependent upon for the existence. There are NO WARS after the initial "rebellious" were brought under control. It's just pure harmony, cooperation, love, peace, and happiness, freedom, justice, and equality. And this is all adding up to what blacks, the original inhabitants of the earth, Mother Earth where all life began and everything comes from the dark in life—everything. And genetic scientific proof has proved it all and scientists continue their evilness here in America behind the scenes, conducting experiments on blacks, perhaps the way following Yacub's orders. And we were already over here in these Americas where Islam has taught the blacks who don't want to go along to get along with the belief of lies they continue to tell, and they have messed up a whole nation of People Who Simply Want Nothing But The Truth ANGELGOONZ

...................**THE END**..................